WEB PAGE
Design

S. Todd Stubbs
Instructional Multimedia Designer
Brigham Young University

Karl Barksdale
Technology Consultant
Highland, Utah

Patrick Crispen
Technology Consultant
Tuscaloosa, Alabama

JOIN US ON THE INTERNET
WWW: http://www.thomson.com   A service of I(T)P®

South-Western Educational Publishing
an International Thomson Publishing company I(T)P®

Cincinnati • Albany, NY • Belmont, CA • Bonn • Boston • Detroit • Johannesburg • London • Madrid
Melbourne • Mexico City • New York • Paris • Singapore • Tokyo • Toronto • Washington

INTERNET

Team Leader: Karen Schmohe
Managing Editor: Carol Volz
Editor: Mark Cheatham
Art Coordinator: Mike Broussard
Technical Editor: Laura Poole, Archer Editorial Services
Production House: Electro-Publishing
Marketing Manager: Larry Qualls
Internal Design: Ann Small
Cover Design: Lou Ann Thesing

ISBN: 0-538-68997-8

4 5 6 7 8 9 10 BM 05 04 03 02 01

Printed in the United States of America

International Thomson Publishing

South-Western Educational Publishing is a division of International Thomson Publishing, Inc. The ITP® registered trademark is used under license.

The names of all commercially available software mentioned herein are used for identification purposes only and may be trademarks or registered trademarks of their respective owners. South-Western Educational Publishing disclaims any affiliation, association, connection with, sponsorship, or endorsement by such owners.

Explore the Web
With these exciting new products from South-Western!

Web Page Design is essential preparation for using any brand of Web page design software, such as Microsoft® FrontPage. Focuses on the Web home page as a practical tool designed to capture an audience. Includes critical analysis of Web page organization, design, and functionality.

- **Web Page Design** by Stubbs, Barksdale, Crispen. 15+ hours of instruction. Essential preparation for using any brand of Web page design software, such as Microsoft FrontPage. Provides a common-sense approach to design fundamentals.
  - Student book, soft cover — 0-538-68997-8
  - Electronic Instructor Package — 0-538-68998-6

Other Complementary South-Western Titles

- **E-Commerce: Business on the Internet** by McLaren and McLaren. 20+ hours of instruction. E-commerce is now an essential course of study for anyone trying to understand today's business climate.
  - Student book, soft cover — 0-538-68918-8
  - Electronic Instructor Package — 0-538-68919-6

- **Understanding & Using the Internet** by Bruce McLaren. 20+ hours of instruction. Provides a comprehensive overview of the Internet from a history of its development to the importance it plays in business today.
  - Student book, soft cover — 0-538-72132-4
  - Electronic Instructor CD ROM — 0-538-72133-2

- **Microsoft FrontPage 2000** by Ciampa. 20+ hours of instruction. FrontPage 2000 allows you to quickly create Web pages without programming.
  - Student book, soft cover — 0-538-69092-5
  - Electronic Instructor Package — 0-538-69093-3

- **Microsoft Internet Explorer 5.0** by Gehris 15+ hours of instruction. Learn the nuts and bolts of the most widely used Internet browser through this excellent introductory text.
  - Student book, soft cover — 0-538-69123-9
  - Electronic Instructor Package — 0-538-69134-4

The Electronic Instructor CD ROM contains tests,
Lesson Plans, solutions, and much more.

Join Us On the Internet
www.swep.com

South-Western
Educational Publishing

The magic of the World Wide Web has caught the imagination of millions of people. What is this magic? How do *you* make this kind of magic?

For some, the magic is having the equivalent of a huge library at their fingertips. For others, it's the ability they have of controlling the screen in a world where the screen often controls them. But for most, it's that they don't have to be a professional magazine publisher, newspaper reporter, graphic artist, or celebrity to get their Web page seen. In fact, unlike other media, you don't have to be "somebody" at all. Everyone can do it!

Design Makes the Difference

That's certainly not to say that everyone can do it *well*. There is a difference between doing it and doing it well. How do people who do it well (make attractive and functional Web pages) do it? What's their secret?

Well, it so happens that it's *not* a secret, and it's *not* magic. It's *design*.

Design is that part of the production of a Web site (or an automobile, or a book, or a work of art, or any creative endeavor) that occurs primarily in the mind of the creator before any part of the physical creation has begun. It is the precursor to all really good creative activity.

A natural inclination for someone creating a new Web site or page is to open an HTML editor and begin writing and inserting tags. Though you certainly will want to know something about HTML before you attempt to develop a complex Web site, making it magic is a function of how much effort you put in to planning *before* the HTML coding starts—in the design.

Creating a Design Document

To guide your work, this thinking we call design must be recorded somewhere. This recorded thinking is collectively called a *design document*. The design document is important if you are doing a Web page all by yourself to help you stay on track. But if you are working with others, it is vital to communicate your creative thinking to them.

That is what this book is about—how to do the design work necessary to create beautiful and purposeful Web sites.

Organization of This Text

In Section One, we cover, in a very general way, the background you should have before beginning to design a Web site, which includes some understanding of how the Web operates and a modicum of knowledge about HTML.

Section Two is the heart of this book. In it, you are introduced to three kinds or "phases" of design: information design, interaction design, and presentation design. You are then guided through the design process using each of these three kinds of design. When you are done, you will have created a design document, which is to a Web page what a script is to a movie.

Section Three provides some of the details you need to understand in order to actually produce the two main ingredients of your Web site: text and pictures.

While this book can stand alone for design instruction, it is greatly complemented by combining it with other texts and courses. We are of the belief that the more you know about the Web, the better your Web pages will be.

Other Sources

Some of the concepts used in this book are a result of reading the book *Interactivity by Design: Creating and Communicating with New Media* by Ray Kristof and Amy Satran (Mountain View, CA: Adobe Press, 1995. ISBN 1-56830-221-5). We highly recommend this delightfully simple and visual book to anyone seriously interested in multimedia design.

Another book you should consider for your library is *Web Style Guide: Basic Design Principles for Creating Web Sites*, by Patrick J. Lynch and Sarah Horton (New Haven, CT: Yale University Press, 1999. ISBN 0-300-07675-4). This is a paper incarnation of a document formerly found only on the Web. Unfortunately, the downloadable version is no longer available. However, a Web-based version can be found at *info.med.yale.edu/caim/manual/*. Lynch and Horton have done a superb job laying out the prerequisites of good Web design.

For Instructors

The Instructor's Package that accompanies this book contains an abundance of materials to help instructors teach this course. Included are lesson plans, chapter tests, and solutions.

The Instructor's Package includes a printed *Instructor's Manual* with an *Electronic Instructor CD-ROM* mounted on the inside back cover. This CD contains everything in the printed instructor's manual along with additional materials on SCANS, different learning styles, building a student portfolio, career materials, and more.

Web Site Support

Because of the nature of the book, it is easier to keep things up to date if you can be linked directly to Web pages that illustrate the best design concepts. Follow these links from this book's Web home page, found at *webdesign.swep.com*. Select the numbered door referred to in the text to see examples of suggested design principles.

Acknowledgments

We are grateful for the contributions of all involved, especially Laura Poole of Archer Editorial Services, David Leiser of Electro-Publishing, and Mark Cheatham, Editor at South-Western Educational Publishing.

As always, thanks to our families, without whom this project would have neither meaning nor the possibility of success.

Using This Book

Activities

Activities are written to support each chapter objective. Each activity begins with a brief explanation of key concepts.

Step-by-Step Instructions provide hands-on reinforcement and simplify the process of working through each activity.

Sidebar Features

Special Features throughout the text present important concepts in a brief, easy-to-read format.

Design Desk

Design Desk features give fledgling Web designers tips for enhancing visual appeal, creating different "looks," and making good design choices in their pages.

JUST THE FACTS

Just the Facts are interesting and informative FrontPage- and Internet-related facts designed to broaden students' understanding of the software and the new medium.

 Design Careers profiles the many exciting web-related career opportunities that are now available.

Design News

Early Edition features peer into the future to anticipate where FrontPage and the Internet might be headed.

Making a Simple Web Page

One of the reasons the Web is so popular is that just about anybody can (and does!) have a Web site. This is because Web sites are relatively easy to create. All you need is a word processor to create your Web pages and someone to host them, that is, make them available on the Internet. The special codes that make the Web work are called **HTML**, which stands for HyperText Markup Language.

Some word processors (like WordPerfect and Microsoft Word) even allow you the option of saving documents as HTML, preserving any formatting you've done to the document. However, for this activity, don't use those options.

1 Open any word or text processor. The built-in Windows text processor (NotePad) or word processor (WordPad) or the standard Macintosh text editor (SimpleText) are fine.

2 Enter the following text exactly as it appears here:

```
<HTML>
<HEAD> </HEAD>
<BODY>
Hello,
my
name
is
[put your name here]
</BODY>
</HTML>
```

Use the "less-than" and "greater-than" symbols (usually found at shift-comma and shift-period, respectively) for the angle brackets.

ACTIVITY 1.4

Objective:
At the end of this activity, you will have created a simple Web page and learned the bare bones of HTML.

Design Desk
Designing for Different Browsers

Because of differences in the way different browsers display a page, many designers will actually create two or more separate versions of every page. The pages then include programming that enables them to tell what kind of browser is requesting the page, and then send the appropriate version. Often, a text-only version is one of those options because it is

 Copy Editor, Proofreader

As more and more major corporations create more and more Web pages and other documents, the need for copy editors and proofreaders has exploded. In fact, many major corporations now have teams of copy editors and proofreaders whose sole job is to edit that company's documents for style, accuracy, flow, and organization.

To be a professional copy editor or proofreader, you will need:
• Excellent English grammar, punctuation, spelling, and proofreading skills
• Ability to work under tight deadlines
• Ability to work well with others on a team
• Working knowledge of the Web, typesetting, graphics, design, and printing.

Most entry-level copy editing jobs require between two and five years of experience coupled with a bachelor's degree in English, composition, journalism, or communications. To gain experience in typesetting, graphics, design, and printing, many professional copy editors or proofreaders start off by working on their high school newspaper or yearbooks, and most go on to work for their college newspaper or yearbook as well.

Figure 2.1
Favorite quotes viewed in
Netscape Navigator

8 Open your Web browser.

9 From the File menu, choose Open, and locate your index.html file. You
may need to click on the Choose File or Browse button in the Open dialog box to be able locate your file.

10 Open your index.html file. Can you view the text in the browser?

Not very exciting, is it? What can we do to spiff it up a little?
We'll answer that in the next activity.

THINKING ABOUT TECHNOLOGY: WEB BROWSERS

Why do you think it is necessary to tell a Web browser that a particular
file is in HTML? Is it possible to use a Web browser to view files other
than Web pages? What do you think would happen if you left the opening or closing HTML tags out of your Web pages?

Design Ethics Linking to Other Sites

As you have seen, it is simple to create a hyperlink to any Web page in the world. But, is it ethical to provide links on your Web pages to other Web sites? The current answer seems to be: "yes that is is fine, provided
the links are not libelous or do not try to pass off one's work as another's." Can you think of any reasons why a
Web site would object to your adding a link to their site on one of your Web pages? Would it be ethical to create
a hyperlink that said "click here to read the mindless drivel of a pack of habitual liars and drug users?" What
would happen to you if you created a link to someone else's work and then wrote "click here for my latest article
on this subject?"

Chapter 2 Hypertext Markup Language

End-Of-Chapter

Vocabulary reinforces the meaning of key terms presented in the text.

Review Questions test retention of important chapter information and serve as an excellent review for the chapter test.

Projects require students to practice the hands-on skills they just learned in the chapter to add to and manipulate the pages they created in the chapter activities.

WEB VOCABULARY

Define the following terms:

1. message
2. audience
3. purpose
4. scope
5. structure
6. random access structure
7. linear structure
8. hierarchical structure
9. mixed structure
10. chunks
11. flowchart

WEB REVIEW

Give a short answer to the following questions, giving specific examples in each:

1. What kind of Web sites would benefit from a random access structure?

2. What kind of Web sites would benefit from a linear structure?.

Wally Woodword owns a small cabinet making business. He creates kitchen and bathroom cabinets and custom wood furnishings for homes. His buyers are homeowners. He uses a variety of woods for his projects. including oak, pine, birch, maple, poplar, and cherry. He wants to sell more cabinets.

Wally feels that if he can create a Web site, he can reach more homeowners. He has asked you to come up with the information design for his new site. Create a short design document for his site. Be creative! If you can impress Wally with your ideas, you may get the job of designing his Web site. Include the following elements:

- Message statement
- Audience statement
- Purpose statement
- Audience Background statement
- Scope
  - This Web site will cover . . .
  - This Web site will not cover . . .
- Flowchart

WEB SITE ▧▧▧ Under Construction Work Teams Ahead ▧▧▧

Working with Wood

Wally Woodword's Wood Works, Inc., faces a great deal of competition. Wally is wondering several things:
1. What other cabinet makers have Web sites?
2. What online resources are available about cabinet making?
3. What information is available about various kinds of wood used in woodworking (oak, pine, birch, maple, poplar, cherry)?

Wally wants a resource list that includes resources on each of these topics. Searching all of this information on the Web might be difficult for one person, but if you divide up the task between three or more team members, the task will be a snap!

As a team, prepare a research list for Wally on each of these three topics.

WRITING ABOUT TECHNOLOGY DESIGN

Having created two design documents, you now understand a great deal about the basics of information design. You have learned how to define the audience, purpose, and the message of a Web site. With what you know about design to this point, write a 100-word answer to one of the three inquiries that follow:

Option 1. Based on what you have learned so far, which element of information design do you feel is the most important to define: the audience, the purpose, or the message? Explain your answer.

Option 2. Explain how the three elements of audience, purpose, and message work together to help organize a great Web site.

Option 3. Why is it helpful to define the scope of your Web site?

Net Project is an ongoing project, in which students build their own business Web site. Students put their new skills to work after each chapter, as they make design decisions and add features to their pages. At the end of the book, they will have a rich professional Web site that reflects their own personal touches.

Web Site Under Construction: Work Teams Ahead is a team option for building the business Web site. Students practice interpersonal skills as they work together toward their common goal.

Writing About Technology emphasizes the importance of developing writing and critical-thinking skills within the emerging, complex world of Web computing. Each of these end-of-chapter assignments provides an opportunity for building a personal portfolio.

CONTENTS

Minimum System Requirements (hardware):

- Windows: Intel 75 Mhz compatible or higher processor
- Macintosh: PowerPC 70 Mhz or higher processor
- RAM for Windows 95/98—24MB minimum (48MB or more preferred)
- RAM for Windows NT—32MB minimum (64MB or more preferred)
- RAM for Macintosh—24MB minimum (48MB or more preferred)
- CD-ROM drive
- Internet access—minimum 9600 bps connection; 28,800 bps or higher recommended
- Printer
- Mouse or other pointing device

Software Requirements

- Microsoft Windows Operating Systems: 95, 98, NT Workstation or NT Server 4 or later with Service Pack 3
- Apple Macintosh Operating Systems: Mac OS 8.1 or later
- Browser: Internet Explorer 4 or later or Netscape Navigator 4 or later
- Minimum 50MB disk space for browser software
- Basic text-editor program (SimpleText, WordPad) and a more sophisticated word-processing program (Microsoft Word, Corel WordPerfect, etc.)
- Bit-map graphics manipulation program, capable of saving in both GIF and JPEG formats (Photoshop, PaintShop Pro, etc.)

Understanding Web Design

In the short span of four or five years the World Wide Web went from a way for scientists and scholars to share scientific papers to a new mass communications medium like television or magazines. In fact, the Web is like a mix between TV and print media: It is made up of mostly text and pictures like a magazine, but you view it on a screen like television (except this screen is connected to your computer).

The Web has become the hottest new way for businesses and individuals to get their message out. Unlike television shows or magazines, creation of a Web page or Web site is relatively cheap and easy—just about anybody can do it. Creating Web pages that are attractive and communicate to the appropriate message, however, is another matter entirely. Good Web pages need to be carefully planned to make them clear, clean, and attractive. This formalized planning process is called design.

When an automobile manufacturer like Ford or Toyota begins to build a car, they don't simply start drilling, cutting, and shaping pieces of metal, welding and bolting them together, putting tires under them, and painting them. Building a car requires careful design. The designers usually start out on paper, then move to small clay models, then to life-sized models, then to prototypes made of plastic and steel, and finally to complete cars. Design starts on paper (or with software) because it is very easy to change things while they are on a sheet of paper. They can make lots of changes without it being too difficult or costly.

Good Web design requires that you know something about the Internet to understand what will work and what won't. In this section you will learn a little about how the Web works, as well as the fundamentals of HTML.

1

What's the World Wide Web?

Chapter Objectives:

In this chapter, you will learn some of the basic functions of the Web. After reading Chapter 1, you will be able to

1. explain what the World Wide Web is and how it works.
2. identify the elements of a Web browser and explain how the browser works.
3. tell what determines how fast a Web page loads.
4. create a simple Web document.

Understanding the World Wide Web

Created by European physicists in the late 1980s, the **World Wide Web** (better known just as "the Web") has rapidly become a powerful communications medium. Through the Web, ordinary people can access millions of informational documents, shop in thousands of online stores, and even share personal information with the rest of the world.

One reason for the recent popularity and explosive growth of the Web is the fact that it is easy to create the files that become a **Web site**. These individual files are known as **Web pages**; anyone with access to a word processor like WordPerfect or an HTML editor like Microsoft FrontPage can easily create dozens of Web pages.

Web pages can be used to sell things, provide news, explain concepts, and share opinions. One reason the Web is so popular is because *anybody* with access to the Internet can look at those Web sites—no matter where they live and no matter where the Web site is located. Through the Internet and the Web, people in virtually every corner of world can now share something about themselves or their interests.

Web Terms

World Wide Web

Web site

Web pages

Internet

URL (Uniform Resource Locator)

Web browser

Web server

packets

hyperlink

search engine

Web index

GUI (graphical user interface)

downloading

modem

HTML

HTTP

HTML tags

How Does the Web Work?

The Web is part of the **Internet**, a global, computer-based communications network. You've probably heard the Internet referred to as the information superhighway (a somewhat overused buzzword). A highway system starts with a neighborhood street that is probably relatively small, but then connects with larger and faster streets until it comes to a freeway or highway. Businesses are often found next to larger streets so they can serve larger numbers of people.

The Internet starts with a simple network, something like a neighborhood of city streets. Computers in a network use the network's connections like streets to send messages and information to each other and share services. Imagine what it would be like if all of the networks in the world were connected together into one giant super network. That is exactly what the Internet is—the interconnection of networks all over the world (not unlike an international highway system).

When you type in the Web address (called a **URL**, which stands for Uniform Resource Locator) of a certain page, your **Web browser** (the program you use to access the Web) contacts the computer where that page resides (the **Web server**). The server receives your message and sends the page by breaking the information up into little bundles called **packets** that each have the address of *your* computer on them. These packets "wander" the Internet, looking for your computer. If one route breaks down, the packets will find another way to reach you. If a packet is lost, your browser will tell the server to send it again. Finally, as all the packets begin to reach your browser, it assembles them into a Web page and displays the page to you.

1. Get together in a small group of about four or five users. On one side of a small piece of paper (about 1/4 of a sheet is fine) write a short note to someone else in the group.

2. When everyone in your group is done writing their notes, tear the notes up into four or five smaller pieces. Don't make the pieces so small they cannot be written on. (These torn-up papers represent packets.)

3. On the back of each torn-up piece of paper, write the name of the person for whom the note is intended. (The name represents the URL.) Place all the pieces in a box or hat or other container with the pieces from everyone in your group.

4. Pass the hat from person to person. Everyone will draw out a "packet" from the hat. If it has your name on it, you can keep it and use it to begin to assemble your note. If not, put it back and pass the hat to the next person.

ACTIVITY
1.1

Objective:
At the end of this activity you will be able to explain what the Web is and how it works.

HOT TIP
Web Tip: What's My Browser?

The instructions and illustrations in this chapter are for Netscape Navigator; they can be easily adapted for use with Netscape Communicator and Microsoft Internet Explorer because they all have basically the same elements. Open your browser by double-clicking on its icon (Macintosh or Windows), or by selecting it from the Applications or Internet categories under the Start menu button (Windows 95 or 98).

As you may have guessed, Internet packets don't really wander aimlessly. Other network computers help send the packets on to their destinations and help locate other routes when one becomes broken or clogged with traffic.

THINKING ABOUT TECHNOLOGY: A HUMAN INTERNET

What would happen if you tried Activity 1.1 with the entire class? How long would it take for every person to receive their packets? How might you modify the activity to allow people to help each other more? How would that make the game more efficient for the whole class?

Net Ethics   *Web Pages that deserve RESPECT*

Everyone knows that there are inappropriate pages floating around cyberspace. As a Web designer, you must consider your ethics or your personal code of behavior as you develop your Web sites.

What will you do if you are asked to develop a Web site containing inappropriate material? This is a difficult question that needs to be answered before this dilemma presents itself. One bit of advice can be found in the term *respect*. RESPECT presents seven mental and ethical tests that you can apply when faced with the important decision of balancing freedom of speech and your ethical behavior. Look for future Net Ethics boxes in which we will investigate all seven tests.

HOT TIP
Web Addresses

Current links to most Web sites presented in this book can be found on the Web Page Design home page at webdesign.swep.com. Remember that a Web address can change at any time. An address given in this book as an example may no longer be valid. If that happens, access this book's home page, or do a search for a similar site.

The Growing Web

In June 1993, there were only 160 Web sites. By April 1998, that number had increased to over 2 million!

Your Connection to the Web—The Browser

Your connection to the Web comes from a type of software called a Web browser that interprets and displays the Web pages to you. In this activity you will learn about how the browser works. (For a complete curriculum on using a Web browser, see *Internet Concepts & Activities* by Barksdale, Rutter, and Rand.)

A Web browser is the software that you use to retrieve and view Web pages. A dictionary definition of *browsing* is "glancing through a book or the books of a library for casual reading." *Browser* is a good name for this kind of software because it allows you to follow **hyperlinks** to see new documents. (Hyperlinks are places in the text or pictures you click on to automatically jump to another page on the Web.) Most other forms of computer access to information require you to either *search* for information or *look it up* in an index. On the Web, you can do those things, too—using a **search engine** like AltaVista to search for Web pages that have things you're looking for, or using a **Web index** like Yahoo! to look up information by category, but it is not the main way you use a browser.

On a browser, hyperlinks to other Web pages are noted by being underlined and differently colored, or set apart in some other way, so you can see them clearly. When your mouse pointer is over these hyperlinks, it turns into a hand to let you know that you can click on them and move to another page. If you decide to return back to the page you just came from, click the Back button (on common browsers, located in the upper left corner of the browser window), and it will jump back. In fact you can jump back several links if you have traveled down several. Eventually, when you get back to where you started, the Back button is shaded gray to let you know you can't click it any more.

In this activity, you will get to know the parts of your Web browser (and what they do), and you will learn to use a search engine and a Web index.

1 Open your Web browser.

2 See how many of the main elements of the browser you can identify, using the following list. If you need help, refer to Figure 1.2a, in which the buttons are clearly labeled.

- The browser's display area

- The address box

- The various navigation buttons

- The status bar

- The animated status icon

- A text-based hyperlink

Design Desk
Designing for Different Browsers

Because of differences in the way different browsers display a page, many designers actually create two or more separate versions of every page. The pages then include programming that enables them to tell what kind of browser is requesting the page, and then send the appropriate version. Often, a text-only version is one of those options because it is viewable on any browser.

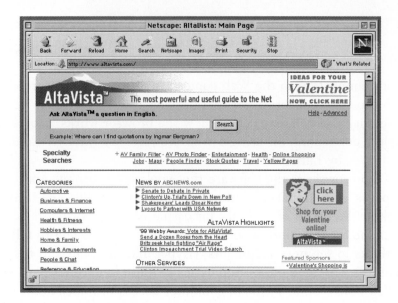

Figure 1.2a
The Netscape Communicator window

3 Type in the following URL:
www.geocities.com.
Take 5 minutes to explore how each of the browser parts work.

Now that you know a little about how your browser works, let's try searching the Web for information. First, we'll go to a true search engine.

4 Click your mouse in the address box. Delete the current contents and type the following URL:
www.altavista.com

5 A page appears (see Figure 1.2a above) with a blank box near the top. Next to this blank box is a button that says Search. This is where you type in what you're looking for. Into this box type the words **web page design** and click the Search button. (Your window might look a little different if you're using Microsoft Internet Explorer or some other Web browser.)

6 After you clicked Search, it brought up a list of pages that match your search criteria. Several of these might be useful to you for this course. Explore them if you like—you can click on the hyperlinks right on the search results page and go to the new pages.

AltaVista and other search engines have records of millions of Web pages, which it compares to the words you entered. If the content of any of them matches the words you typed, it puts them in a list for you.

Now let's look at a Web index. One of the most popular Web indexes is Yahoo!

7 Click your mouse in the address box. Delete its current contents and type the following address or URL:
www.yahoo.com
and then press Return or Enter.

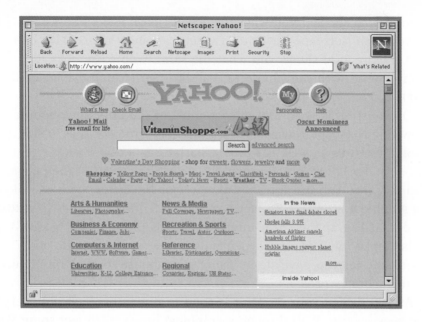

Figure 1.2b
The Yahoo! Web page

8 You will see the page shown as Figure 1.2b. You can search this one, too, but we're not going to. Instead, click on the link titled "WWW" under the "Computers & Internet" category. Now see if there is a category called "Design" and click on that.

Unlike AltaVista, which automatically gathers information about pages on the Web, Yahoo! lets users like you advertise their Web pages by asking Yahoo! to list them. That is why we call it an index rather than a search engine. You can find information by browsing through the topics and subtopics.

An overwhelming majority of Web users use either Netscape Navigator or Microsoft Internet Explorer as their browsers, but there are, in fact, over fifty different Web browsers available today. Many of these browsers work very differently, so a Web page that looks great in one browser might look completely different in another.

JUST ≡ FACTS

Why Does the Internet Work that Way?

The scientists who invented the Internet made it so that the self-addressed packets can find their way to your computer even if one or more of the "highways" is broken down. Why? This protocol was invented for the military during the cold war when the United States and Western Europe were concerned that the Soviet Union might start a nuclear war. The scientists wanted to make sure that messages got through even if there was a nuclear attack. That's one of the reasons the Internet is so flexible.

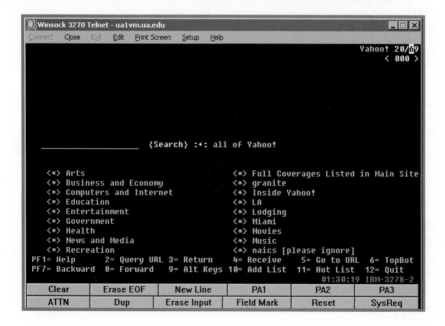

Figure 1.2c
The Yahoo! Web page viewed with the Charlotte Web browser

Figures 1.2b showed you what the Yahoo! page looks like when viewed with Netscape Navigator (which can show images). In contrast, Figure 1.2c shows you what the same Web page looks like when viewed with the Charlotte Web browser (which displays only text).

Obviously this is an extreme example of the difference between browsers. Netscape Navigator is a *graphical browser* that is able to display pictures as well as words. Charlotte is a *text browser* that can only display words. Fortunately, over 87 percent of the people who surf the Web use Internet Explorer or Navigator, both of which are graphical browsers. In fact both Internet Explorer and Navigator have a **GUI** (graphical user interface; GUI is pronounced "gooey"). GUIs display pictures and other multimedia (such as audio and video) and let you navigate by using your mouse to click on pictures or highlighted words.

As you design your pages, it is good to remember that not everyone accesses the Web through a graphical browser. In fact some Web surfers—such as visually impaired surfers who use text-based browsers with text-to-speech software to "read" the Web pages to them—will not be able to see any of the pictures on your Web pages.

THINKING ABOUT TECHNOLOGY: SEARCH ENGINES OR INDEXES

Which do you think is a better way to look for particular information on Web pages—a search engine or an index? Might you use one for one purpose, and one for another? What purposes?

JUST THE FACTS

Using the Internet for More that Just the Web

Just like the highway is not used just for cars, but for buses, trucks, and semi-tractor trailers, the Internet is the "highway" for lots of different kinds of services. One of these is *e-mail* (think of it as a mail truck or delivery service). Another is *FTP* (File Transfer Protocol), which is used to send large files across the Internet.

The Web is only one of many uses of the Internet, although at present, it is by far one of the largest and most popular. The Web uses a protocol or tranfer method called HyperText Transfer Protocol (or HTTP—which is why all Web addresses start with "http://")

Design News

Good News from Cupertino

What is the number one computer used to develop Web pages? The Apple Macintosh. Because Web pages are often developed by graphic artists, and the Macintosh is the most popular computer platform for the graphics and multimedia industries, it is also number one in Web development.

In addition, over half the digital video content avaialable on the Web uses Apple's QuickTime technology.

How Fast Is the Web?

ACTIVITY

1.3

Objective:
After this activity you will be able to tell what determines how quickly a Web page loads.

Because computing happens at the speed of electricity, it usually doesn't take long for the Internet packets to find their way to your computer. This process is called **downloading**—the process of transferring files from one computer to another, usually from the Web server to a browser's computer. However, if there is a lot of traffic on the Internet or if your connection to the Internet is slow, you may have to wait while these packets reach your computer.

The time it takes for someone to download a page over the Web is a function of four factors:

- the size of the Web page (including the text, all graphics, and so on),

- the speed of the user's Internet connection,

- the speed of the Web server and its connection, and

- the amount of Internet traffic or other messages competing for use of the Internet.

Typically, the user's Internet connection is the slowest of these, so the faster the user's Internet connection, the faster the Web pages will load. The bad news is that over 60 percent of current (1998) Internet users access the Web through very slow Internet connections.

In contrast, if the members of your intended audience are at a large company, a university, or at some public schools, they may have a more direct connection to the Internet, which is much faster. In our street analogy, it's as if they have an office right off the highway. A lot of people access the Web (especially from their homes) with a **modem**, which greatly restricts download speed. A modem is a device that lets computers use telephone lines to communicate, but they are often quite slow. Some telephone and cable companies are beginning to offer new, faster services to the Web like digital connection lines and cable modems. Obviously, the faster the user's connection, the faster they will be able to download your page.

1. Open your browser.

2. Type the following address in the address box, but do *not* press Return or Enter: *webdesign.swep.com/act1-3a.html*. Using a watch or clock with a second hand, start timing when you press the Return key and see how long it takes for this page to load. Write the approximate time.

3. Do the same thing for the following address. Type it in the address box, but again, do not press Return or Enter: *webdesign.swep.com/act1.3b.html/*. Now time how long it takes this one to load after you press the Return key. Write the approximate time.

4. Note the difference in the downloading times. What is the difference between these pages? Why did the first page load faster?

As a Web page designer you have no control over the user's connection. You usually cannot change the server's speed or how much Internet traffic there is. That leaves the *size of your page* as the only thing you can control to affect speed. The more things you put on your Web page and the larger it is, the longer it takes to download—and people hate to wait. So, the longer it takes to download, the smaller your audience will be. After a while, impatient users will simply give up waiting for your page and go off to visit another site.

That means that as a Web designer, you are left with a complicated decision: "Which will increase the size of my viewers—using this really cool graphic in my site, or doing away with the graphic so it will download faster?" Often the answer is a compromise between the two: a smaller graphic or a more Web-friendly way to accomplish the same "coolness."

THINKING ABOUT TECHNOLOGY: WHAT CAN YOU CONTROL?

Which of the four factors affecting download time can you as a Web page designer control? Which ones, if any, can the person who browses your Web page control? Which one is the hardest for anybody to control?

JUST THE FACTS

Just the Facts: Mosaic and Netscape

The world first graphical Web browser was called Mosaic. It was developed in 1993 by the National Center for Supercomputing Applications (NCSA) by students and professors at the University of Illinois, Urbana-Champaign. Mosaic took the Internet by storm. Within a few months of its release, over 2 million people were using it, and Web traffic had increased by over 300,000 percent! One of the students who helped develop Mosaic, Marc Andreessen, left the university in 1994 to start a new company called Mosaic Communications. When the people at NCSA complained that they owned the name Mosaic, Andreessen changed the name of the company to Netscape.

Making a Simple Web Page

One of the reasons the Web is so popular is that just about anybody can (and does!) have a Web site. This is because Web sites are relatively easy to create. All you need is a word processor to create your Web pages and someone to host them, that is, make them available on the Internet. The special codes that make the Web work are called **HTML,** which stands for Hypertext Markup Language.

Some word processors (like WordPerfect and Microsoft Word) even allow you the option of saving documents as HTML, preserving any formatting you've done to the document. However, for this activity, don't use those options.

1 Open any word or text processor. The built-in Windows text processor (NotePad) or word processor (WordPad) or the standard Macintosh text editor (SimpleText) are fine.

2 Enter the following text exactly as it appears here:

```
<HTML>
<HEAD> </HEAD>
<BODY>
Hello,
my
name
is
[put your name here]
</BODY>
</HTML>
```

Use the "less than" and "greater than" symbols (usually found at shift-comma and shift-period, respectively) for the angle brackets.

3 Save this document in text-only format giving it a file name that ends in ".html" ("dot H-T-M-L"; a period in Web addresses and file names is pronounced "dot.")

4 Open your browser, and use it to view your newly created page. It should look like Figure 1.4a.

Figure 1.4a
Your sample Web page

Notice that the file's address in the address box does not start with the usual "http://" but rather starts "file://" because it came from a local disk. (**HTTP** stands for Hypertext Transfer Protocol, the transfer method for Web pages.) Also notice that in spite of the fact that you put every word on a separate line, it all shows up on the same line in the browser.

Though it is a very simple example, all Web pages are fundamentally like this one. They are all made up of text with simple codes inserted that tell the browser how to display the information. The codes in the less than and greater than symbols are called **HTML tags**. HTML is called that because you "mark up" the text with these tags. In Chapter 2 you will learn more about using these tags to create your site.

THINKING ABOUT TECHNOLOGY: WHAT'S DESIGN?

If creating Web pages is so simple, why do we have a whole book about designing good ones? Brainstorm what the differences might be between a good Web page (a well-designed one) and a poor one.

Web Milestones

The First Hypertext Machine

When was the first hypertext machine thought of? Would you believe 1945? Vannevar Bush conceived of a device, called "Memex," which used photographic technology to link related materials together in what today we call *hypertext*. Though it was never built, the device is the great-grandmother of the Internet, which is based on hypertext. The word *hypertext* was not thought of until much later—by Ted Nelson in the 1960s.

WEB VOCABULARY

Define the following terms:

1. World Wide Web
2. Web site
3. Web pages
4. Internet
5. URL
6. Web browser

7. Web server
8. packets
9. hyperlink
10. search engine
11. Web index
12. GUI

13. downloading
14. modem
15. HTML
16. HTTP
17. HTML tags

WEB REVIEW

Give a short answer to the following questions:

1. Why is it important for a Web designer to understand how the Web works?

_____

_____

2. What is the difference between a Web search engine and a Web index?

_____

_____

3. What can you as a Web page author do to make sure that a page loads quickly?

_____

_____

_____

4. When using a word processor to build a Web page, what precautions would you have to take?

_____

_____

_____

WEB SITE UNDER CONSTRUCTION

As a newly hired Web designer for World Wide Widgets, Inc., you have been given the assignment to investigate making Web pages for the company. The boss, Wendy Widmark, is kind of old-fashioned and is hesitant to move into advertising on the Web. Before she will approve of developing Web pages, she has to understand how the Web works.

Use or additional sheets of paper to write a memo to Wendy, detailing how the Web works. Also, create a simple Web page for World Wide Widgets to demonstrate to Wendy how Web pages are built.

WEB SITE ///// Under Construction Work Teams Ahead /////

Form a team of three or four users to work together to build Web pages. Pretend that you could have people from any kind of background or training. What kinds of people would you choose? What does the creation of a Web site entail? With your team brainstorm all the kinds of skills you can think of, that might be needed to build the site. Then have team members select a job title that would be responsible for each one. Possibilities include an artist, a graphic designer, a computer programmer, a systems analyst, a videographer, a sound engineer, an information designer, a project coordinator, and others.

Have each member of your group decide which they would want to be, and discuss what you all think that person does and why their contribution to Web page development is important.

WRITING ABOUT TECHNOLOGY: Why Have a Web Site?

With what you know about the Web at this point, write a 100-word essay to one of the following questions:

Option 1.   How important is it for a business to have a Web site?
Option 2.   How important is it for a school to have a Web site?
Option 3.   How important is it for an individual to have a Web site?

_____
_____
_____
_____
_____
_____
_____
_____
_____

Hypertext Markup Language

Chapter Objectives:

In this chapter, you will understand how to turn your text into Web pages using HTML. After reading Chapter 2, you will be able to

1. format text using basic HTML formatting tags.

2. add white space to Web pages by using paragraphs, line breaks, and horizontal rules.

3. organize information using bulleted lists and numbered lists.

4. use hyperlinks to link Web pages to other Web pages around the world.

An HTML Primer

Despite the bright colors, fancy graphics, and impressive multimedia, a Web page is nothing more than a text file with formatting codes inserted. In spite of the advertising you may have heard or seen suggesting the need for fancy Web authoring programs or elaborate HTML editors, you really only need a word processor like Corel WordPerfect or Microsoft Word to create visually stunning Web pages that are focused on the needs of your audience. Even simple text editors like SimpleText (Macintosh) or WordPad (Windows) can be used to create great Web pages.

The only trick to making your pages viewable on any Web browser, regardless of software or type of computer, is making sure that you follow the rules or standards for formatting Web pages. The standard formatting language on the Web is HTML, which stands for Hypertext Markup Language. In fact, the terms *HTML file* and *Web page* are synonymous.

In this chapter you will learn, step by step, how to convert the plain text file(s) into real Web pages that can be viewed by any Web browser. Welcome to the world of Web pages!

Web Terms

hard-coding

containers

start tag

end tag

white space

physical style

logical style

unordered list

ordered list

hyperlink

anchor tag

Design Careers

Copy Editor, Proofreader

As more and more major corporations create more and more Web pages and other documents, the need for copy editors and proofreaders has exploded. In fact, many major corporations now have teams of copy editors and proofreaders whose sole job is to edit that company's documents for style, accuracy, flow, and organization.

To be a professional copy editor or proofreader, you will need:
- *Excellent English grammar, punctuation, spelling, and proofreading skills*
- *Ability to work under tight deadlines*
- *Ability to work well with others on a team*
- *Working knowledge of the Web, typesetting, graphics, design, and printing.*

Most entry-level copy editing jobs require between two and five years of experience coupled with a bachelor's degree in English, composition, journalism, or communications. To gain experience in typesetting, graphics, design, and printing, many professional copy editors or proofreaders start off by working on their high school newspaper or yearbooks, and most go on to work for their college newspaper or yearbook as well.

Basic HTML Coding

Now you'll learn how to turn that text into a real Web page. In spite what you may have heard, you *don't* have to be a computer guru to be able to do this. A Web page is nothing more than a simple, text-only document, and anyone with access to a word processor can create a Web page in no time.

Figure 2.1a shows some text I keyed in using Microsoft Word. These are some of my favorite quotes.

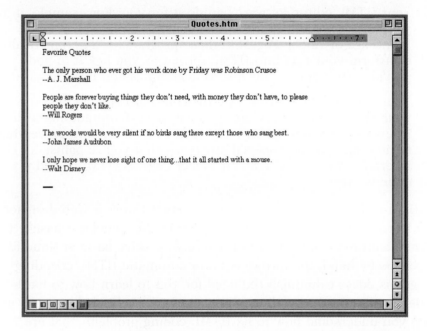

Favorite Quotes

The only person who ever got his work done by Friday was Robinson Crusoe
--A. J. Marshall

People are forever buying things they don't need, with money they don't have, to please people they don't like.
--Will Rogers

The woods would be very silent if no birds sang there except those who sang best.
--John James Audubon

I only hope we never lose sight of one thing...that it all started with a mouse.
--Walt Disney

Figure 2.1a
Four favorite quotes in Microsoft Word, no tags

Now, you may be wondering how to turn plain text like Figure 2.1a into a sharp-looking, interesting Web page. We'll add HTML to make it viewable in a Web browser.

The Wonderful World of HTML

To turn the text of these quotes into a Web page, we first have to add some special markup codes to it. These markup codes are called HTML tags, and they are instructions to Web browsers on how they should format and display the various parts of a Web page. HTML tags let you change the background color of your pages, add extra spaces between paragraphs, display some words in boldface (or italics, or underlined, and so on), center parts of your text, and even create links to other Web pages. Text without HTML tags is much like text from a manual typewriter—functional, but boring. You can view it in a Web browser, but it's not particularly interesting.

As important as HTML tags are, though, chances are you have never seen what they look like. That's because HTML tags are invisible to the audience. The tags are just instructions to a Web browser, telling it how it should display a particular Web page. In other words, Web browsers read and interpret HTML tags; they don't display them.

Transforming Your Text Documents into HTML Files

There are three ways you can transform your text documents into HTML files:

1. You can insert the HTML tags into your document by hand. This is known as **hard-coding**.

2. Your HTML editor software can do it for you. For example, if you write your text in a Web editor program like Microsoft FrontPage or Adobe PageMill, these programs will automatically transform your text into HTML format as you key it in and provide other options for inserting graphics and hyperlinks.

3. Your word processor can do it for you. For example, if you write your text in Microsoft Word, you can have Word automatically insert the necessary HTML tags into your document, preserving formatting and most special attributes that you've painstakingly inserted. From the File menu, select Save as HTML… and it's done for you.

Hard-coding is one of the most important things a Web designer can learn to do. Just as the introduction of the calculator hasn't eliminated the need for you to learn how to solve basic arithmetic problems by hand, the introduction of automatic HTML encoding programs doesn't diminish the need for you to learn how to hard-code. Besides, understanding what is going on behind the scenes will help you understand how to fix HTML coding problems that are bound to occur as you design your own Web pages.

Basic HTML Tags

HTML tags are not difficult to learn and use. In fact, *each* HTML tag has three basic parts:

1. an open angle bracket (which is just a less than sign): <

2. the text and characters that tell Web browsers what to do

3. a closing angle bracket (which is just a greater than sign): >

For example, the HTML tag to add a title to the top of your Web page is <TITLE> (we'll talk about this tag in depth in a few moments). Notice how the open bracket, the word *TITLE*, and the closing bracket all combine to create the <TITLE> tag.

HTML is not case sensitive, so <TITLE>, <title>, and <TiTlE> all do the same thing. However, since capital letters stand out more than lowercase letters, all of the HTML tags in this book are written in uppercase.

Many HTML tags are also used in pairs (sometimes called **containers** or paired tags). The first tag, called the **start tag**, tells the browser where to turn on particular formatting function (like italics);

the second tag, called the **end tag**, tells the browser where to turn off the function. The only difference between a start tag and an end tag is that the end tag has a forward slash in it immediately following the opening bracket. For example, the <TITLE> tag tells the browser where the title starts, and the </TITLE> tag tells the browser where the title ends. By the way, the reason HTML tags like <TITLE> and </TITLE> are called containers is because they modify everything that is *contained* between them.

Now that you know the basics of an HTML tag, let's start using some HTML tags to create Web pages. In fact, let's hard-code the text you saw in Figure 2.1a.

A third thing to know about HTML tags is that they have to be LIFO. LIFO stands for "last in first out." It means that the *last* tag you turn on should always be the *first* you turn off. Put another way, when one set of tags are inside another, imaginary lines connecting the start tags to their end tags must never cross. To determine whether they are crossed, draw a line from the start tag and end tag of each of the sets of tags used. Look at Figure 2.1b to see improperly and properly nested tags.

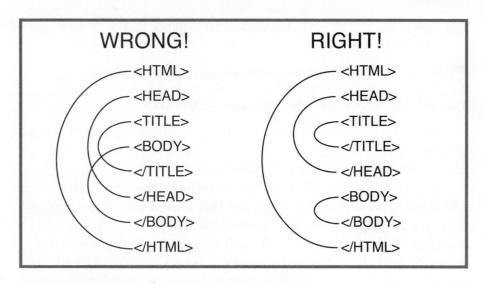

Figure 2.1b
Improper and proper HTML tag nesting

The Three Sections of an HTML Document

As you design and create your Web pages, you should know that every HTML file has three main sections (as the bare basics):

1. the HTML document

2. the HEAD section

3. the BODY section

In fact, here is the outline of tags you will use for *every* Web page that you design (we have indented them to make it easier to see the nesting):

```
<HTML>

    <HEAD>
      <TITLE> Your page's Title </TITLE>
    </HEAD>

    <BODY>
       Your page's main information
    </BODY>

  </HTML>
```

Now let's explain what all of this means.

The HTML Section: <HTML> and </HTML>

The first tag in each and every HTML document is <HTML> and the last tag is </HTML>. This will *always* be the case.

The <HTML> tag at the beginning of an HTML files tells the Web browsers that all of the stuff following the <HTML> tag should be treated as a Web page. The </HTML> tag tells the browser where the page ends.

1 Type in the text shown in the window on Figure 2.1a in your word processor.

2 Mark up the text with the opening and closing <HTML> tags.

The HEAD Section: <HEAD> and </HEAD>

The HEAD section immediately follows the opening <HTML> tag. You turn on the head section with the opening <HEAD> tag, and you turn it off with the closing </HEAD> tag.

The purpose of the HEAD section is to provide general information about a particular Web page, but this information is not actually displayed in the page's body. Think of the head section as the cover of a book. It gives the book's title and may even tell you about the author or provide a brief synopsis of the book's content. The HEAD section of a Web page tells Web browsers what the page's title is (using the <TITLE> tags), and it may also share information with search engines about the page's content and keywords (using special comment tags, which we will discuss in a later chapter).

In our favorite quotes example, the HEAD section would be

```
<HEAD>
<TITLE>Favorite Quotes</TITLE>
<HEAD>
```

For now, the only thing you should place in your HEAD section is your Web page's title. The title should be placed between the starting and ending <TITLE> tags, and it is important that you choose a title that clearly describes your page's topic. In addition to displaying the first sentence of your Web page, most search engines also display your page's title. If you choose a poor or confusing title, your page's traffic will be low and your potential audience might not be able to find you.

When your audience views your Web page, your page's title will appear at the top of their browser window, in the title bar just above the menu bar.

3 Mark up your text in your word processor with the opening and closing <HEAD> and <TITLE> tags.

The BODY Section: <BODY> and </BODY>

The BODY section follows the head; this is where you place *all* of your Web page's content (text, pictures, and so on). In effect, your Web page's content is everything between the starting and ending BODY tags.

4 Mark up the text for famous quotes in your word processor with the opening and closing <BODY> tags.

Putting It All Together

Figure 2.1c shows you the famous quotes marked up with all of the basic HTML tags. Notice where each of the tags is placed. You will use this same basic framework in every HTML file you create.

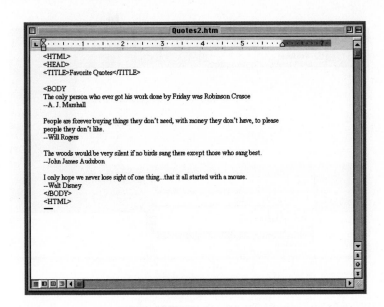

```
                            Quotes2.htm
      · · · 1 · · · · 2 · · · · 3 · · · · 4 · · · · 5 · · · · · 6 · · · · 7 · ·
<HTML>
<HEAD>
<TITLE>Favorite Quotes</TITLE>

<BODY>
The only person who ever got his work done by Friday was Robinson Crusoe
--A. J. Marshall

People are forever buying things they don't need, with money they don't have, to please
people they don't like.
--Will Rogers

The woods would be very silent if no birds sang there except those who sang best.
--John James Audubon

I only hope we never lose sight of one thing...that it all started with a mouse.
--Walt Disney
</BODY>
<HTML>
```

Figure 2.1c
Basic HTML mark-up of famous quotes

That's all there is to it. Add these basic HTML tags to the text and you've created the bare bones of a Web page!

Important Stuff!

Before you move on to the more sophisticated HTML coding, you need to remember to save every Web page you create as a *plain text file* (rather than a word processor document; we'll show you how to do that in a moment). If you save your Web page as anything other than a text document, you may not be able to open and view it in a Web browser.

You also need to remember to save every Web page you create as *filename*.**html** or *filename*.**htm.** The .html or .htm extension is a code that tells Web browsers that your file is coded in HTML.

Finally, be sure to save your main Web page as **index.html.** When a Web server is called without a specific file name, the first file the server usually tries to download is called *index.html*. If you save your main Web page as *index.html,* you help ensure that it is the first page your audience will see.

Saving and Viewing Your Web Page

As you can see, creating a simple Web page isn't particularly difficult. Saving and viewing your new Web page, however, can be a little trickier.

5 Now that you've marked up the text, from your word processor's File menu, choose Save As... (Your word processor may also have a Save as HTML... option, but you have already marked up your text by hand, so you can ignore it.) Choose Save As...

6 In the Save As... dialog box, choose the file type Text Only with Line Breaks and then name your file *index.html* (choose the file type first, *then* name the file). Figure 2.1d shows you the Save As dialog box in Microsoft Word.

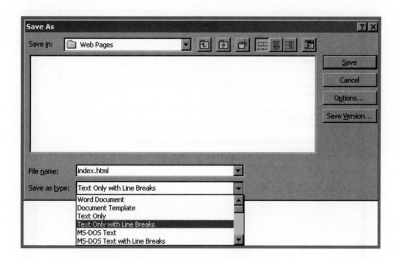

Figure 2.1d
Saving a file as Text Only with Line Breaks in Microsoft Word

7 Save your index.html file and remember where you save it. You might want to create a new folder named Web Content and keep all your Web files there.

After you have added the basic <HTML>, <HEAD>, <TITLE>, and <BODY> tags to your document, you can view your new page in your Web browser. Figure 2.1e shows what our favorite quotes page looks like in Netscape Navigator.

8 Open your Web browser.

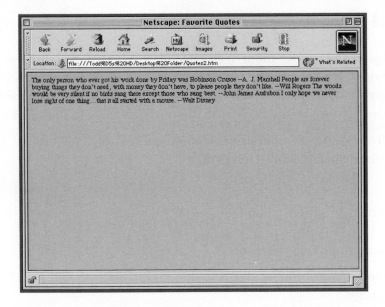

Figure 2.1e
Favorite quotes viewed in
Netscape Navigator

9 From the File menu, choose Open, and locate your index.html file. You may need to click on the Choose File or Browse button in the Open dialog box to be able locate your file.

10 Open your index.html file. Can you view the text in the browser?

Not very exciting, is it? What can we do to spiff it up a little? We'll answer that in the next activity.

THINKING ABOUT TECHNOLOGY: WEB BROWSERS

Why do you think it is necessary to tell a Web browser that a particular file is in HTML? Is it possible to use a Web browser to view files other than Web pages? What do you think would happen if you left the opening or closing HTML tags out of your Web pages?

ACTIVITY

2.2

Objective:

In this lesson, you will learn how to add white space to your Web page's text to increase readability.

Add White Space

One of the quirks about Web page design is that Web browsers are stupid. By default, the software reads the text of your Web pages as a continuous line of single-spaced text. For example, you could deliberately key in the body text of your Web page to look like this:

> This Web page contains the complete text of
> Abraham Lincoln's Gettysburg
>   Address.
>
> Four   score   and   seven   years   ago
>   our
> fathers brought forth on …

When a Web browser displays this text, though, it will look like this:

> This Web page contains the complete text of Abraham Lincoln's Gettysburg Address. Four score and seven years ago our fathers brought forth on …

The browser ignores all of your extra spaces and returns and displays your text as continuous, single-spaced lines.

Adding White Space

Take another look at Figure 2.1e, the favorite quotes Web page we created in the last activity.

Not very readable, is it? One of the reasons this Web page is so unattractive is that it doesn't have a lot of **white space**. *White space* refers to the amount of empty space on a page. If your pages have a lot of white space, they will be easier to read and will make a stronger impression on your audience. In fact, a rule of good Web page design is **the more white space, the better**.

How can you add white space to your Web pages when Web browsers ignore the extra spaces you put into your body text and display your text as a continuous line? Well, you can force the browsers to break your body text up by using the paragraph tag, line breaks, and horizontal rules.

Paragraphs: <P> and </P>

To add white space between each of your paragraphs, use the <P> tag. At the beginning of every paragraph in your body text, put a starting <P> tag. At the end of every paragraph, put an ending </P> tag. Figure 2.2a shows you the favorite quotes HTML file with the paragraph tags added, and Figure 2.2b shows you what our new Favorite quotes Web page looks like in Netscape Navigator.

That looks much better! Notice that the Web's definition of a paragraph is a little different than the definition used in books and other publications. When you start a new paragraph in a book, you usually indent the first sentence of that paragraph. On the Web, the

Design Desk

</P>?

Is the ending paragraph tag (</P>) really necessary? This issue is the subject of many debates, and the answer is both yes and no. The official word from the World Wide Web Consortium (W3C) is that the </P> tag is optional. However, as you will learn in Activity 2.4, to center portions of your Web page's text, the </P> tag is essential. Since not using the </P> tag could cause you difficulty when you try to align portions of your text, your best bet is to always use the </P> tag at the end of your paragraphs. Good habits will prevent problems down the road.

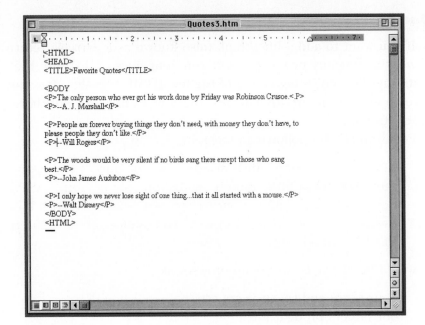

Figure 2.2a
HTML mark-up of quotes with
<P> tags inserted

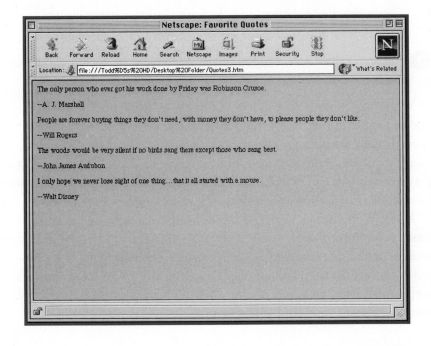

Figure 2.2b
The new, improved favorite
quotes viewed in Netscape Navigator

first sentence of a paragraph is not indented. Instead, the paragraph
tag simply inserts a space between each paragraph, significantly increasing the page's white space.

1 Using your word processor, open the favorite quotes HTML file you
began hard-coding in Activity 2.1.

2 Add some white space to the Web page by coding the text with
paragraph tags where necessary.

Line Breaks: \<BR\>

If you want to add a line break (also known as a carriage return) *without* adding any new space between your lines of text, use the \<BR\> tag. The \<BR\> tag is one of the few HTML tags that does not have an ending tag. In other words, there is a \<BR\> tag, but there is no \</BR\> tag.

For example, the following paragraph

```
<P> Four score and seven years ago <BR> our
fathers brought forth <BR> on this continent a
new nation, <BR> conceived in Liberty, and
dedicated to the proposition <BR> that all men
are created equal. </P>
```

would be displayed in a Web browser as.

Four score and seven years ago
our fathers brought forth
on this continent a new nation,
conceived in Liberty, and dedicated to the proposition
that all men are created equal.

3 Add some white space to the quotes Web page by coding the text with line break (\<BR\>) tags where necessary or desired.

While the paragraph tag (\<P\>) inserts a blank line between each line of text, the line break tag (\<BR\>) does not. Also notice that even though we added extra spaces to our text—in this example, there is a space both before and after each of the \<BR\> tags (just for easy readability when looking at the code)—Web browsers automatically display only one space between each word.

Many Web page designers forget about this "feature" and needlessly try to cram all of their Web page text and HTML codes into as small a space as possible. Good Web page designers use the one-space feature to their advantage. Compare the following HTML example with the one given above. As a Web page programmers, which one is easier to read and understand?

```
<P>
Four score and seven years ago <BR>
our fathers brought forth <BR>
on this continent a new nation,<BR>
conceived in Liberty, and dedicated to the
proposition <BR>
that all men are created equal.
</P>
```

When you hard-code your HTML, feel free to add spaces or returns anywhere you think it is necessary. The Web browsers will ignore your extra spaces and only pay attention to your HTML codes and your body text, automatically putting exactly one space between each of your words.

Horizontal Rules: <HR>

Occasionally, you may want to add a horizontal line, or rule, to the body of your Web page. The <HR> tag lets you do this. These lines can visually break your page into sections, but it is easy to get carried away. The best Web page designers use horizontal rules only sparingly.

4 Add some white space to the quotes Web page by coding the text with horizontal rules where necessary—but use them sparingly.

In our favorite quotes page, a good place to add a horizontal rule is between each of the quotes, like this

```
P>--A. J. Marshall</P>
<HR>
<P>People are forever buying things they don't
need, with money they don't have, to please
people they don't like.</P>
```

Figure 2.2c shows you how this horizontal rule would appear in Netscape Navigator.

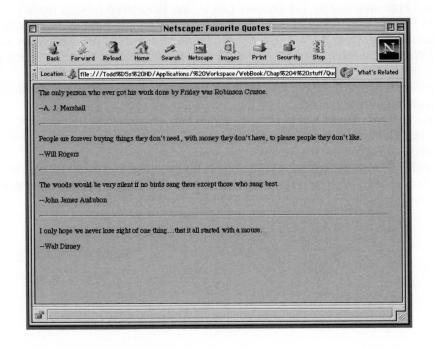

Figure 2.2c
Horizontal rule in favorite quotes

Like line breaks, horizontal rules do not need to be turned off—there is no ending </HR> tag.

Putting White Space to Work for You

Obviously, adding white space with paragraph tags, line breaks, and horizontal rules dramatically increases the readability of a Web page.

5 Save your HTML file (remember, save your file as Text Only with Line Breaks).

6 Launch your Web browser and view the Web page. Experiment some more with the file and see what you like, viewing in your browser as needed. Is the text easy to read?

THINKING ABOUT TECHNOLOGY: WHITE SPACE

Why do you think white space makes a Web page easier to read? What would happen if your pages have too little white space? What would happen if your page had too much white space? How could adding too many horizontal rules make your Web pages difficult to read? Why do you think line breaks and horizontal rules don't require ending tags?

JUST THE FACTS

HTML "Flavors"

Is there only one official set of HTML tags? Yes.
The Web and HTML were was both invented by Tim Berners-Lee in late 1990 while he was working at CERN, the European Particle Physics Laboratory in Geneva, Switzerland. The first "official" HTML tags were the ones created by Berners-Lee. Over the years, the responsibility for drafting new standards for HTML tags has fallen to the World Wide Web Consortium (W3C), an international organization headed by Berners-Lee.

Many Web browser companies feel that the W3C's list of HTML tags is limiting, so these companies have created new HTML tags that are only recognized by their particular browser. For example, Netscape invented a <BLINK> tag that causes text to blink. Unfortunately, the <BLINK> tag doesn't work in rival Web browsers such as Internet Explorer or Opera (and, to be completely honest, blinking text can be extremely annoying).

The problem with using unofficial, browser-specific HTML tags is that you are effectively telling your audience that if they don't use a specific Web browser, they should go away. Obviously, you don't want to do this. That is why all of the HTML tags in this book come straight from the W3C's list at *www.w3.org.*

ACTIVITY
2.3

Objective:
In this lesson, you will learn how to modify your Web page's text using physical and logical style tags and headings.

In addition to letting you add white space, line breaks, and horizontal rules to your Web pages, HTML tags let you modify the way your Web page's text will actually appear to your audience. Specifically, you can change your text's **physical style** and **logical style**.

Physical Styles

Physical style refers to how your Web page's text actually appears to your audience. For example, I can change the physical style of the last half of this sentence by **specifying that its text be displayed in bold**. By bolding all of the words in the last half of that sentence, I changed the way that sentence appears—I modified its physical style.

There are HTML tags that will let you display text on your Web page in bold, italics, underlined, and other styles. These tags let you change the physical appearance of your Web page's text. Table 2.3a shows you some of the most popular physical style tags.

Physical Style Tag	What it Does
<B> </B>	Specifies that the enclosed text should be displayed in boldface.
<I> </I>	Specifies that the enclosed text should be displayed in an italic font.
<U> </U>	Specifies that the enclosed text should be displayed as underlined.
**	Specifies that the enclosed text should be displayed as a subscript, as in the number 2 in H_2O.
**	Specifies that the enclosed text should be displayed as a superscript, (as in the number 2 in $E = mc^2$.
<TT> </TT>	Specifies that the enclosed text should be displayed in monospaced or a fixed-pitch typewriter font.
<BIG> </BIG>	Specifies that the enclosed text should be displayed using a big font (compared with the current font).
<SMALL> </SMALL>	Specifies that the enclosed text should be displayed using a small font (compared with the current font).

Table 2.3a
Physical style tags (information compiled from Ron Woodall's HTML Compendium at *htmlcompendium.org*)

Design Desk *Use Restraint*

Many new Web page designers get carried away with physical style tags and horizontal rules, using as many of each as possible. Remember, you should only use those tags that make your pages appealing to your audience (remember them?). If your pages are cluttered with unnecessary markups, your message could get lost.

For example, the following HTML code

```
<P>

Four score and seven years ago our fathers
brought forth on this continent, <I> a new
nation</I>, conceived in Liberty, and
dedicated to the proposition that <B> all
</B> men are created equal.
</P>
```

would generate the following display:

Four score and seven years ago our fathers brought forth on
this continent, *a new nation*, conceived in Liberty, and
dedicated to the proposition that **all** men are created equal.

1 Using your Web browser, open the favorite quotes HTML file you began
hard-coding in Activities 2.1 and 2.2.

2 Use your word processor to insert the bold (<B>) and italics (<I>) tags
to change the physical style of portions of your Web page's text.
Experiment until you find the combination you like best.

You can also combine physical style tags, such as bold and italics:

```
<P>
Four score and seven years ago our fathers
brought forth on this continent, <B><I> a new
nation</I></B>, conceived in Liberty, and
dedicated to the proposition that all men are
created equal.
</P>
```

If you do combine style tags, remember to turn off *both* tags
when you are through. If you don't, the rest of your text will run in
bold or italics, whichever one you forgot to close. Forgetting to turn
off a physical style tag is one of the simplest mistakes a Web
designer can make. In fact, a great way to learn about physical style
tags is to create a dummy Web page that uses each of the tags.
Experiment with different combinations of physical style tags and
deliberately leave off a few ending tags to see what happens.

Logical Style Tags

While physical style tags let you change the appearance of parts
of your text, logical style tags let you change the way parts of your
text are actually used. For example, when you quote a long passage
in a paper or report, you are supposed to indent the quote on both
sides. In effect, you are changing the way that particular text is used
by setting it apart from the rest of the text in your paper or report.

The focus of logical style tags is to change how portions of your text are supposed to be used, not how your text is supposed to appear. If you want to change your text's *appearance*, use physical style tags only. Table 2.3b shows you some of the more popular logical style tags.

Logical Style Tag	How It Is Used
<EM> </EM>	*Used to indicate an emphasized phrase. It is typically rendered as italics.*
<STRONG> </STRONG>	*Used for text that requires a strong emphasis. It is usually displayed in bold font.*
<BLOCKQUOTE> </BLOCKQUOTE>	*Used for long quotations that require format changes in the form of an indent, both left and right.*
<CITE> </CITE>	*Used to indicate the title of a book or other citation. It is usually presented in italics.*
<CODE> </CODE> or <KBD> </KBD>	*Indicates text that should be keyed in by the user. It is usually presented in a typewriter font.*

Table 2.3b
Popular logical style tags (information compiled from Ron Woodall's HTML Compendium at *htmlcompendium.org*)

③ Experiment with different logical style tags to see how they affect the content of the favorite quotes page.

For example, assume that you want to set off a long quote in your Web page so that it was are clearly a quotation. You don't want to mislead your audience into thinking that *you* wrote those particular sentences, so you might set them apart from the rest of the Web page with the <BLOCKQUOTE> tag. In other words, your HTML would look like this:

```
<P><BLOCKQUOTE>People are forever buying
things they don't need, with money they don't
have, to please people they don't
like.</BLOCKQUOTE></P>
<P>--Will Rogers</P>
```

This would generate the following display:

> People are forever buying things they don't need, with money they don't have, to please people they don't like.
>
> --Will Rogers

Chances are you won't use logical style tags as much as you use physical style tags. In fact, one of the shortcomings of logical style tags is that different Web browsers interpret and display them differently. While a physical style tag like bold (<B>) is displayed the same way in most browsers, logical style tags like emphasis (<EM>) appear differently from browser to browser. The thing to remember is that you should never use a logical style tag only to change the appearance of your text. Logical style tags should be used to change the way your text is *used*. Try experimenting with different logical style tags to see what happens.

Headings: <H1> </H1> to <H6> </H6>

The HEADING tag is a tool that lets you organize your Web page's content by emphasizing your major topics. For example, imagine if your Web page's content is:

```
Presidents of the United States
George Washington
Washington served from 1789-1797
John Adams
Adams served from 1797-1801
Thomas Jefferson
Jefferson served from 1801-1809
```

Clearly, some of these items are more important than others. Imagine if you were asked to write this text in outline form, but weren't allowed to indent any of the text. What would you do? Chances are, you'd change the size of each line of text depending on that line's importance. You want certain lines to stand out more than others.

That's what the HEADING tag does. The HEADING tag gives you the ability to create up to six levels of headings, from high—<H1>—to low—<H6>. For example, here is one way to add headings tags to our sample text.

```
<H1>
Presidents of the United States
</H1>
<H2>
George Washington
</H2>
<P>
Washington served from 1789-1797
</P>
<H2>
John Adams
</H2>
<P>
Adams served from 1797-1801
</P>
<H2>
Thomas Jefferson
</H2>
<P>
Jefferson served from 1801-1809
</P>
```

Figure 2.3a shows what this would look like in Netscape Navigator.

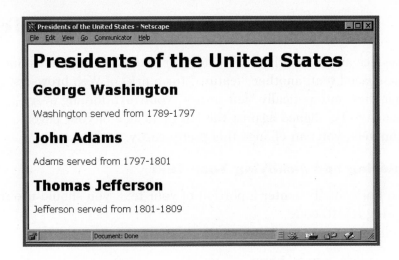

Figure 2.3a
Netscape Navigator, showing the use of the <H1> and <H2> tags in the presidents list

4 Add some headings to your favorite quotes file where appropriate. (You may have to make up some text for this.)

Wow, what a difference that makes! HEADING tags are very much like logical style tags. You should never use a HEADING tag only to change the appearance of portions of your text. They should be used to indicate the hierarchy of the topic header.

Modifying Your Web Page's Text

The best way to find the physical and logical style tags that will improve the appearance of your Web page is to experiment with the different tags and see which ones you like.

5 Now that you've made changes to the favorite quotes Web page, save your file and preview it in your Web browser to make sure you like what you see. If not, adjust and experiment until you get a result you like.

It is not uncommon for Web designers to modify the physical appearance of their pages several times before they find the right combination of tags.

THINKING ABOUT TECHNOLOGY: MODIFYING TEXT

How are physical style tags similar to the font formatting functions of your favorite word processing program? Why should you *not* use logical style tags simply to change your text's appearance? Considering the display differences associated with logical style tags, can HTML be described as a "what you see is what you get" type of language? Why?

Objective:

In this lesson, you will learn
how to align your Web
page's text and how to
organize your text using lists.

Align and Organize Your Text

Besides automatically displaying your text as a continuous line of single-spaced text, another "feature" (or quirk) of Web browsers is that they automatically "left justify" your text, forcing every sentence to be aligned against the left-hand side of your page. Fortunately, you can change this pretty easily.

Centering and Justifying Your Text

To horizontally center a portion of your text, you should use the following HTML code:

```
<P ALIGN="CENTER">
 your text here
</P>
```

Notice that this is just a regular paragraph tag with a few things added to it. Also notice that these extra things are *only* added to the start tag.

To right-justify a portion of your text (to force all of the sentences in a particular portion of your text to be aligned against the right-hand side of your page, making a ragged left edge), you should use:

```
<P ALIGN="RIGHT">
 your text here
</P>
```

Can you figure out what the HTML code is to left-justify your text? Actually this is a trick question. The answer is

```
<P>
 your text here
</P>
```

Remember, by default Web browsers automatically left-justify your text unless you tell the browsers to do otherwise. So, the <P ALIGN="LEFT"> is redundant and unnecessary.

Want to play with justification? Take a stab at the activity below.

1 In your word processor, key in the sentence "Four score and seven years ago our fathers brought forth on this continent, a new nation, conceived in Liberty, and dedicated to the proposition that all men are created equal."

2 Copy this sentence twice (hint: use you word processor's cut-and-paste function). You'll have three copies of the sentence.

3 Hard-code this document with the appropriate <HTML>, <HEAD>, <TITLE>, and <BODY> tags, using "Alignment Test" for the title.

4 Hard-code the first sentence so that it is centered.

5 Hard-code the second sentence so that it is right-justified.

6 Hard-code the third sentence so that it is left-justified.

7 Save this document as *align.html*.

8 Launch your Web browser.

9 Open your align.html document, and see what happens.

Now that you know how to justify your text, let's look at how you can organize your text using lists.

Lists

In Activity 2.2, we talked about the importance of adding white space to your Web pages. Besides using paragraph and line break tags, a great way to add white space to your Web pages while also clearly organizing your information is to use *lists*. For example, if you were writing a page about the first presidents of the United States of America, it would be silly for you to write

```
The first five Presidents of the United
States, in order, were George Washington
(1789-1797), John Adams (1797-1801), Thomas
Jefferson (1801-1809), James Madison (1809-
1817), and James Monroe (1817-1825).
```

when you could just as easily (and more attractively) write

```
The first five Presidents of the United
States, in order, were
```
- George Washington (1789-1797),
- John Adams (1797-1801),
- Thomas Jefferson (1801-1809),
- James Madison (1809-1817), and
- James Monroe (1817-1825).

By putting this information in a list, it is much easier to read, and, because of the additional white space, it looks better, too.

The two main types of lists you will be using in your Web pages are **unordered lists** (or bulleted lists) and **ordered lists** (or numbered lists).

Unordered Lists

If you have a list of items that have no specific order, use an unordered (or bulleted) list. The HTML tags for an unordered list are <UL> and </UL>. Each item in your list has to be identified with a list item tags: <LI> and </LI>.

1 Open your word processor and create a new document.

2 Key in the ingredients for a peanut butter and jelly sandwich.

<P ALIGN= "JUSTIFY">?

The World Wide Web Consortium (W3C) recognizes the <P ALIGN="JUSTIFY"> tag, but neither Netscape Navigator or Internet Explorer recognize it yet. In other words, while it is theoretically possible for you to justify your text in HTML, most Web browsers will only allow you to center, right-justify, or left-justify your the text (and both Netscape Navigator and Internet Explorer automatically read <P ALIGN= "JUSTIFY"> as <P ALIGN="LEFT">).

3 Hard-code the document with the appropriate <HTML>, <HEAD>, <TITLE>, and <BODY> tags, and use the title "How to Make a Peanut Butter and Jelly Sandwich."

4 Create an <H1> heading titled "Ingredients."

5 Turn the text of the ingredients section into an unordered list (<UL>) and make each ingredient a list item.

The following is an example of how to hard-code the list of presidents using the <UL> and <LI> tags:

```
<P>
   The first five Presidents of the United
   States, in order, were
</P>
<UL>
   <LI>George Washington (1789-1797),</LI>
   <LI>John Adams (1797-1801),</LI>
   <LI>Thomas Jefferson (1801-1809),</LI>
   <LI>James Madison (1809-1817), and</LI>
   <LI>James Monroe (1817-1825).<LI>
</UL>
```

Figure 2.4a shows you how this appears in Internet Explorer.

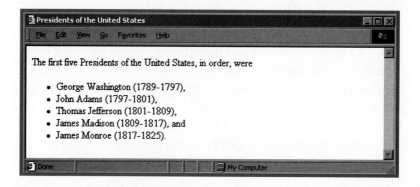

Figure 2.4a
The presidents list as an unordered list in Internet Explorer

Ordered Lists

If you have a list of items that have a specific order, use an ordered (or numbered) list. The HTML tags for an ordered list are <OL> and </OL>. The list item tags are identical to the ones used from unordered lists: <LI> and </LI>. With an ordered list, the numbers are inserted automatically, so you don't need to input the numbers by hand.

6 After the ingredients section, key in the preparation instructions for making the peanut butter sandwich (listing all the steps you need to take, in order).

7 Create an <H1> heading titled "Preparation" above the instructions.

8 Turn the text of the preparation section into an ordered list (<OL>) and code each step with the <LI> tags.

9 Save your document as *recipe.html*.

10 Open your recipe.html file in your Web browser and view it.

The following is an example of how to hard-code the list of presidents using the <OL> and <LI> tags:

```
<P>
   The first five Presidents of the United
States, in
   order, were
</P>
<OL>
   <LI>George Washington (1789-1797),</LI>
   <LI>John Adams (1797-1801),</LI>
   <LI>Thomas Jefferson (1801-1809),</LI>
   <LI>James Madison (1809-1817), and</LI>
   <LI>James Monroe (1817-1825).<LI>
</OL>
```

Figure 2.4b shows you how this appears in Internet Explorer.

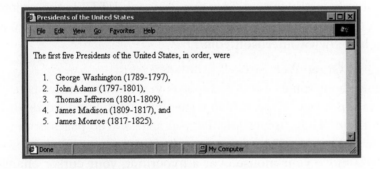

Figure 2.4b
The presidents list as an ordered list in Internet Explorer

THINKING ABOUT TECHNOLOGY: LISTS

How do lists make your Web pages easier to read? Could you use lists to organize information on essays and written tests? What benefits or drawbacks do you think would come from using lists on essays or reports? How would an instructor react to an essay or written test that utilized white space?

Spell Check Your Tags!

When a Web browser encounters a tag it does not understand, it simply ignores it.

ACTIVITY

2.5

Objective:

In this lesson, you will learn how to add hyperlinks to your Web page's text.

Adding Hyperlinks

What makes the Web so popular is the ability to jump from Web page to Web page around the world just by clicking your mouse on a highlighted word or image, called a **hyperlink**. To understand how hyperlinks work and how to add hyperlinks to your Web pages, you first have to understand **URLs** (Uniform Resource Locators).

URLs

Think about all of the computers connected to the Internet. Now add in all of the files that are stored on all of those computers. Mind-boggling, isn't it? Imagine how difficult it would be for you to find one specific file on one specific computer if there wasn't some sort of universal guide or addressing system.

Fortunately, such an addressing system exists. Every single file on the Web has its own unique address, called a Uniform Resource Locator or URL. The format of a URL is

protocol://server address/path/filename

For the most part, the "protocol" in your URLs will be HTTP, which stands for Hypertext Transfer Protocol. HTTP is the protocol used to transfer Web pages across the Internet; a sample of a Web URL is **http://www.microsoft.com/.**

Linking to Other Web Sites

Think about some of the Web pages you have recently seen. Chances are, most of these Web pages had highlighted words or images in them. These hyperlinks let you access Web pages around the world with just the click of a mouse. In fact, in many Web browsers, when you move your mouse over a hyperlink, your cursor changes from an arrow to a pointing hand (try it!).

After a while, you'll want to add hyperlinks to the Web pages that you develop. To add a hyperlink to your Web page, you use the following HTML code:

```
<A HREF="URL"> your text </A>
```

This is called the **anchor tag** (<A>). "HREF" stands for Hypertext Reference, which is just a fancy way of saying it points to a Web page. An anchor tag creates a link to another Web page somewhere in the world.

The *URL* part of the anchor tag is where you should put the full URL (including the "http://" part) of the site you wish to link to, and *your text* is where you put the text that you want to be highlighted as the clickable link. For example, assume that your Web page has the sentence "For more information, visit Yahoo!" and you want to make it so that the words "visit Yahoo!" are a link to Yahoo!'s Web site (*www.yahoo.com*). Here is how you would hard-code that sentence:

```
<P>
For more information,
<A HREF="http://www.yahoo.com"> visit Yahoo!</A>
</P>
```

That's it! Figure 2.5a shows you what this looks like in Netscape.

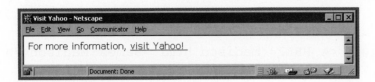

Figure 2.5a
Viewing a link in Netscape

1. Using your word processor, open up the quotes Web page created in Activity 2.1.

2. Add a few lines suggesting that visitors look for more Famous quotes at sites like Excite (www.excite.com), Bookwire (www.bookwire.com), or Merriam Webster (www.m-w.com).

3. Add the necessary codes to create hyperlinks to these other Web sites.

4. Save your index.html file, and open it in your browser. The hyperlinks should appear blue and underlined.

5. Test the new hyperlinks by clicking on them and seeing if they take you where they should. (You'll need to be connected to the Internet to do this.)

By the way, you should *always* remember to use an ending anchor tag (</A>). If you don't, all of the text of your page will be a hyperlink!

Local Links

Local links are just links to other Web pages on your Web site. In Activity 2.4, we created an ordered list of the first five presidents. What if you have created five different Web pages—washington.html, adams.html, jefferson.html, madison.html, and monroe.html—and you want to create an list with items that linked the presidents' names with their own individual pages? You'd use the following HTML code:

```
<P>
   The first five Presidents of the United
   States, in order, were
</P>
<OL>
<LI>
     <A HREF="washington.html">George
     Washington</A>
     (1789-1797),
</LI>
```

```
<LI>
    <A HREF="adams.html">John Adams</a>
    (1797-1801),
</LI>
<LI>
    <A HREF="jefferson.html">Thomas
    Jefferson</a>
    (1801-1809),</LI>
<LI>
    <A HREF="madison.html">James Madison</A>
    (1809-1817), and
</LI>
<LI>
    <A HREF="monroe.html">James Monroe</A>
    (1817-1825).
<LI>
</OL>
```

This may look complicated, but it really isn't. It is simply the ordered list we created in Activity 2.4 with the addition of a few anchor tags. Notice that you don't have to specify a full URL for the individual files, because they are on the same server (this is known as a *relative URL*). Figure 2.5b shows you what this hyperlinked list looks like in Netscape.

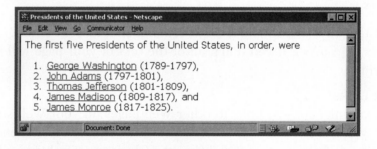

Figure 2.5b
Hyperlinked presidents list in Netscape

6 Add local links on your peanut butter and jelly sandwich Web page.

7 Create small HTML files that just include the name of each ingredient with proper tags.

8 Save your files. Now open the main sandwich recipe list and test the local links.

THINKING ABOUT TECHNOLOGY: LINKS

How are hyperlinks similar to bibliographies and works cited lists? In what ways could the use of links have helped you when you wrote your last paper or report? In what way would links have helped your readers verify your sources?

As you have seen, it is simple to create a hyperlink to any Web page in the world. But, is it ethical to provide links on your Web pages to other Web sites? The current answer seems to be: "yes that is fine, provided the links are not libelous or do not try to pass off one's work as another's." Can you think of any reasons why a Web site would object to your adding a link to their site on one of your Web pages? Would it be ethical to create a hyperlink that said "click here to read the mindless drivel of a pack of habitual liars and drug users"? What would happen to you if you created a link to someone else's work and then wrote "click here for my latest article on this subject?"

CHAPTER REVIEW

WEB VOCABULARY

Define the following terms:

1. hard-coding

2. containers

3. start tag

4. end tag

5. white space

6. physical style

7. logical style

8. unordered list

9. ordered list

10. hyperlinks

11. anchor tag

WEB REVIEW

Give a short answer to the following questions:

1. Why should new Web designers learn to hard-code?

2. What are the two main divisions of a Web page?

3. Name three ways you add white space to your Web pages and how they differ.

4. Why do you not have to use the <P ALIGN="LEFT"> tag to left-justify your text?

5. Why should you not use logical tags to change the appearance of your Web page's text?

WEB SITE UNDER CONSTRUCTION

One of the best resources for Web training is the Internet. Use your Web browser to visit *builder.cnet.com/Authoring/Basics/* and read the following tutorials:

- learn the basics
- set up the page
- let's talk text
- add some links
- create a list

WEB SITE ///// Under Construction Work Teams Ahead /////

Explore the Web pages you have created and look for any additional changes you think your audience would appreciate (white space, physical style changes, text alignment, lists, and so on). Think about how you can use these HTML tags to their best effect as you get ready to design Web pages that are more complex. As you create more Web pages, remember to give your HTML files meaningful names so you can easily remember what the files are.

WRITING ABOUT TECHNOLOGY: HTML Coding

With what you know about Web design at this point, write a 100-word answer to one of the following:

Option 1. Explain why you think hard-coding is or is not an essential skill for new Web designers to learn.

Option 2. How could using browser-specific HTML codes affect your audience? Why do Web browser companies create new HTML codes that only work in their browsers?

_____

_____

_____

_____

Design Ethics   *RESPECT the Web: The Responsibility Test*

The Responsibility test encourages Web page designers to assume a personal responsibility for the Web pages they create. No single person, group, company, or government agency owns or controls the content of the Web. It is up to Web designers to ensure that the Web is a people-friendly place for information, entertainment, and learning.

Your main responsibility is to make sure that the Web site you design adds to the value of the Web as a communications resource. Don't allow unprofessional or unethical pages to appear on a Web site that you design. This can be a difficult professional task, but by keeping your ethics in mind and designing your pages so that they conform to your value system, the task can become much easier.

Web Design Fundamentals

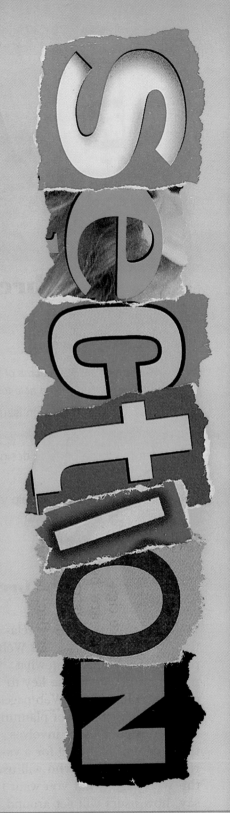

Great Web sites are not built by individuals, they are built by teams with members that possess three essential skills:

1. writing skills
2. programming skills
3. artistic skills

It is nearly impossible to find a single person who can write well, is a great artist, and can program interactive Web pages using tools such as JavaScript, Dynamic HTML, or Java. Instead, companies that need a great Web site will hire several people with differing skills and abilities and expect them to work as a team to accomplish the goals they have established for their Web site.

To keep all of these talented people working together effectively, **design documents** are created. A design document is to a Web site as a script is to a movie—it guides the action. A design document outlines the goals of the site, including all of the individual sections and interactions that need to be considered as the Web site is created. Design documents are built around three critical design issues:

1. information design
2. interaction design
3. presentation design

Interestingly, information design often requires a team member with writing skills. Interaction design requires that at least one team member possess great programming skills. Presentation design usually requires a person with artistic skills. The blending of writing, programming, and art with information, interaction, and presentation design are the keys to the creation of a successful Web site.

A design document coordinates teams of talented people and the three critical design issues. It keeps writers, programmers, and artists working together efficiently. In this section we will explore information, interaction, and presentation design. In the process, we will show you how to create a design document to keep all of the complicated actions performed during the Web site development process moving forward.

In Chapter 3 we will provide an overview of the three aspects of design. In Chapter 4, we will focus in on the specifics of information design. Chapter 5 will demonstrate interaction design. Finally, Chapter 6 will demonstrate how to integrate presentation design into your Web projects.

Three Parts of Web Design

Chapter Objectives:

In this chapter you will learn some of the primary concepts of Web design. After reading Chapter 3, you will be able to:

1. critically evaluate design issues by comparing and evaluating Web pages.

2. learn the three parts of design and the issues that go with each of them.

3. ask questions that will help you learn the information you need to guide your design tasks.

Web Terms

design

information design

interaction design

presentation design

message

audience

purpose

structure

organization

navigation

interactivity

color scheme

font

graphics

layout

Elements of Great Web Page Design

Creating Web pages is relatively easy. Creating *great* Web pages, however, is somewhat more complicated. The key to creating outstanding Web pages is a specialized kind of planning called **design**. Design involves thinking and planning for a variety of issues, like who will use the Web page, what you want to say, how users will get around, and how it will look.

Web design is divided into three parts:

1. **Information design**

2. **Interaction design**

3. **Presentation design**

The design process is best done in the order listed above—first you determine the general information, its purpose, and structure; then you decide how to organize it. Only when you have made these decisions can you decide how the Web site should look.

Many Web designers make the mistake of changing the order of these steps by deciding how the site will look first. Although this might help you see results quickly, it often means that the site needs to be reworked considerably after you know more about who it is for or how it will work.

Design Evaluation

ACTIVITY

3.1

Objective:
In this lesson, you will
develop critical thinking skills
by evaluating Web pages.

In this activity you will exercise your "design muscles" by comparing several Web pages. As you visit each Web page or site, consider what you do and don't like about each one.

Even at this early stage in your Web page designing career, trust your instincts! You already know what you like and don't like about some Web pages. Your ideas about what makes a good page will be valuable to you as you proceed through these activities.

To start with, look at Figure 3.1a below.

Figure 3.1a
Microsoft's Web page

Ask yourself the following questions about the figure above:

- What do you like and dislike about this Web page?

- What information does this page share?

- Does it appear to be easy to find important or pertinent information?

- Is the information well presented?

Next, you're going to visit two "live" Web sites and see what the businesses who sponsor them are doing to make their sites easy to use, informative, and fun to visit.

1 Load your Web browser and point it to: *webdesign.swep.com*

2 Find the *Doorways to Design* link. There you will see two hyperlinks, *Door Number 1* and *Door Number 2*. Each link will take you to a different Web page.

3 Visit and read the pages behind Door Number 1 and Door Number 2.

4 Answer the following questions about the Web page behind Door Number 1. Write short, 15- to 35-word answers for each question on a separate sheet of paper.

- What do you like about this Web page?
- What do you dislike about this Web page?
- What information does this page share?
- Is it easy to find important or pertinent information?
- Is the information well presented?
- Does the page provide interesting links that take you to other, related Web pages? Where do the links take you?
- Does this page get you involved in some way? If so, how?
- Are the graphics and multimedia effects interesting and exciting? Explain why or why not.

5 Answer the following questions about the Web page behind Door Number 2.

- Do you like this page any more or less than the Web page behind Door Number 1? Explain why or why not.
- What information does this page share?
- Is the information well presented?
- Does the page provide interesting links to other parts of the Web site? If so, where do they lead?
- Does this page get you involved in some way? If so, how?
- Are the graphics and multimedia effects interesting and exciting?

THINKING ABOUT TECHNOLOGY: GOOD DESIGN

You already have a sense of what a great Web site should be like. If you had to teach someone else how to judge a Web site, what qualities would you tell them to look for? In your mind, what makes a great Web page?

SCOOP

By 2002 there will be 200 million people creating Web pages of some sort. Many of these people have been called "microcontent" providers. *Microcontent* is information that may only be of interest to a few people. A microcontent provider may be someone like you, who posts information about your interests or answer questions others may have online.

Information Design

ACTIVITY

3.2

Objective:
In this activity, you will examine the basic concepts of information design.

As we mentioned before, the process of Web design can be divided into three parts:

1. Information design

2. Interaction design

3. Presentation design

When designing Web pages, you need to consider each of these three parts in some detail. The best place to start is with *information design*. (Later, in Activities 3.3 and 3.4, we will get into interaction and presentation design.)

When you do information design you think about what you want to tell about, whom you're going to tell it to, what things they already know, why you want to tell it, and how the information will be put together. Knowing the answers to these questions is a necessary foundation to everything else you need to understand to create high-quality Web design.

For example, consider the Internal Revenue Service Web site (*www.irs.gov*), shown in Figure 3.2a. Given how people often feel about paying taxes, it is important that this government site be easy to use and very informative. Because tax information can be very confusing, information design and information management are critical for the IRS. The IRS doesn't want a bunch of frustrated tax payers visiting their Web site, so they try and make their site as simple as possible, but as informative and helpful as it can possibly be. Notice how the opening page is friendly, simple, and leads the viewer in.

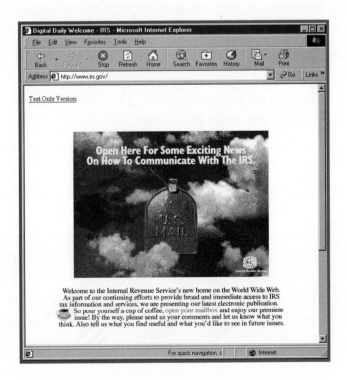

Figure 3.2a
The IRS Web site makes paying taxes a little less painful

Information Design

There are five things to think about in the process of information design:

- **Message:** What information do you wish to share?

- **Audience:** Whom do you wish to share your message with?

- **Purpose:** How and why do you want to share your message with this audience?

- **Background:** What does your intended audience already know about the subject you are discussing?

- **Structure:** How can your message be organized most effectively?

When you answer these questions, you provide essential guidelines to creating interesting and informative Web pages. Consider the IRS Web page example. Their message is clear: "We are here to help you complete your tax obligation." Their audience includes any taxpayer online. Their purpose is to see that taxes are paid properly. The background experience of the IRS Web site audience will vary. Some taxpayers will be very informed; others will be confused about the entire process. When you click on the mailbox shown in the figure, a host of options appears that helps structure the message for taxpayers with a variety of backgrounds.

In the next few steps you will identify how others have wrestled with these questions and discover how they have successfully or unsuccessfully delivered their message. By reverse-identifying a Web site's audience, message, purpose, background, and structure, you will learn how important these issues are to developing a good Web page.

1 In your Web browser, return to *webdesign.swep.com* and select *Doorways to Design*. Select the link that says *Door Number 3*.

2 Answer the following questions in 15 to 35 words on another sheet of paper.

- What is the primary message of this Web page? What is this organization trying to communicate?

- Whom do you think this organization's message is directed to? Who would want to know this information?

- Why do you think this organization wants to share this information? What do they have to gain?

- Did you already know something about this organization before you visited this Web site? If your answer is *yes*, explain what you knew. What new things can you learn at this site?

- Do you think the message this organization wants to share is organized in such a way that it is easy to read or follow?

Did the pages behind Door Number 1 and Door Number 2 have a clear message? For whom are these pages created? Do they address the issues related to audience, purpose, structure, message, and background?

In 1998 the Web reached its first 100 million users. By 2003 the number is expected to rise as high as 320 million. Do you think there is a ceiling to the number of people that can be connected to the Web at any one time?

From the Archives

Internet Portals

Internet portals sprang up all over the Web between 1994 and 1999. A portal allows quick and easy access to large amounts of Internet information. You can also search topics at portal Web sites. Probably the first super portal was Yahoo! It has been called a *super portal* because it records millions of hits every hour. For most of the relatively short history of the Web, Yahoo! has been one of the most popular places for Web surfers to begin their Web wanderings.

Yahoo! was created in 1994 by two Stanford University students, David Filo and Jerry Yang. It quickly became a multi-million-dollar business. Other super portals followed Yahoo!'s lead, including Excite, Go, Snap, AltaVista, and many others. These portals make the Web accessible and easy to navigate.

ACTIVITY

3.3

Objective:
In this lesson you will examine interactivity on Web pages.

Interaction Design

Interaction design, even on a single Web page, is concerned with how the information will be organized on the page, how people will find their way around your Web site, and how people will work with the information on your site. Interaction design is concerned with what cues or guidelines you will give them for getting around without getting lost.

Interaction design looks at three essential things:

- **Organization:** How are the graphics, text, and other elements arranged on the page?

- **Navigation:** Are there any links or buttons on the home page that make it easy to move to other parts of the Web site?

- **Interactivity:** Do you have a chance to interact or to participate in the Web pages in some way? Are you expected to do something with the information on this Web site?

The site that pioneered interaction design is probably Yahoo! (see Figure 3.3a). Yahoo! was the first super portal, or access point to the Web. They made finding information easy.

Figure 3.3a
Yahoo! pioneered Web interaction in 1994

Design Desk *Doing Things in Order*

Design is best done in order—first, you determine the general information (information design), its purpose, and structure; then you decide how to organize it (interaction design). Only when you have made these decisions do you decide how the Web site should look (presentation design).

Many people make the mistake of changing the order of these steps by deciding how the site will look first.

In this activity, you will visit and analyze other sites that provide doorways to the Web. By reverse-identifying issues in interaction design, you will learn just how important this phase of design is to developing good Web pages.

1 In your Web browser, return to *webdesign.swep.com* and select *Doorways to Design*.

2 Select the link that says *Door Number 4* and compare this Web site with *Door Number 3*.

3 Answer the following questions in 15 to 35 words on a separate sheet of paper.

- Which Web site's overall organization do you like the best? Explain why.
- What types of navigation tools (that is, buttons, contents list, site index) do each of the Web sites use? Which ones do they have in common?
- Which of these two sites has you participating or making the most decisions? What kinds of decisions or interactions are expected of visitors to this site?

THINKING ABOUT TECHNOLOGY: INTERACTION

In your experience, what types of Web sites do you like to visit and why? Do you like active sites or do you like to sit back and watch powerful media effects? What elements would you like to incorporate your own favorite Web elements into your Web pages?

Net Ethics — rESPECT the Web: The Everybody Test

The Everybody test asks a simple question: "Will everybody who has access to a Web site that you design appreciate it or enjoy it?" If you feel that some people may be offended by a specific Web page, you need to consider changing the page to make it more acceptable to your audience.

The Everybody test is easy to administer. If you have any questions about how your Web page may be received by certain members of your audience, ask them! Ask visitors what they think of the content and imagery of your page; ask them to look at it. Let them express their opinions. Then, show them you value their opinions and comments and make the positive changes they suggest.

ACTIVITY

3.4

Objective:

In this activity, you will
consider different Web site
presentation styles.

Presentation Design

Presentation design is sometimes called visual design. Presentation design helps you plan how your Web site will actually look. There are three elements to consider are **color scheme**, **fonts**, and **graphics**. The arrangement and coordination of these elements on Web pages creates a great-looking page.

Naturally, a site that represents the Château de Versailles, one of the world's greatest displays of eighteenth-century grandeur, would be expected to make an outstanding visual or artistic impression (see Figure 3.4a). Note the simple, striking graphic on the home page. But what about sites with a more commercial or business tone?

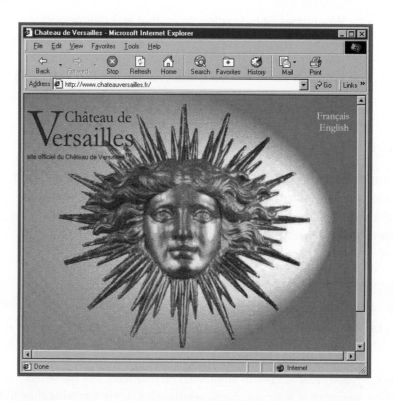

Figure 3.4a
The Château de Versailles Web page opens virtual doors to some of the greatest artwork in history

The following questions are the issues to keep in mind for presentation design:

- **Color scheme:** What colors should you use for the background, text, and links on your page?

- **Font selection:** What style of letters do you want—simple or fancy, large or small?

- **Graphics selection:** What pictures or graphic elements do you want to appear on the page?

- **Multimedia effects:** Are there any multimedia motion or sound effects that you wish to include on your page?

- **Arrangement:** Where on the page should you place your graphics, text, or multimedia effects (known as **layout**)?

1 In your Web browser, return to *webdesign.swep.com* and select *Doorways to Design.* Select the link that says *Door Number 5*.

2 Answer the following questions in 15 to 35 words on a separate sheet of paper.

- What colors has this company chosen for background color? written text? hyperlinks? hyperlinks that have been followed?

- Is the font easy to read? Do the font's letters have little tails or extensions (known as serifs) or are they straight (known as sans serif)? Which one of these examples is closer to the font style?

    Serif Letters

    San serif Letters

- Describe the graphics used on the Web site. Do they add to the Web site's message, or do they distract from what the company is trying to accomplish?

- Are there any special effects—sound, movies, animation, or special motion effects—that contribute to the Web site?

- Are all the elements (font, text, graphics, and effects) arranged on the page in such a way that each element adds to the page? Which, if any, elements are hard to notice or difficult to see? What is the dominant element on the page, that is, which element stands out the most?

THINKING ABOUT TECHNOLOGY: PRESENTATION

Of the five pages behind the first five doors, which one do you think arranges its elements the most effectively? Why?

SCOOP

Many of today's most popular games can be played live over the Web. You can pick your opponents from anywhere in the world and compete in real time. If you were designing a Web site for game players, what would you put on your games site?

WEB VOCABULARY

Define the following terms:

1. design
2. information design
3. interaction design
4. presentation design
5. message

6. audience
7. purpose
8. structure
9. organization
10. navigation

11. interactivity
12. color scheme
13. fonts
14. graphics
15. layout

WEB REVIEW

Give a short answer to the following questions:

1. Describe your goals during the information design phase.

2. Describe what is involved with interaction design.

3. What is the purpose of doing presentation or visual design?

4. Why are all three phase of design important? Why should you do them in order?

DESIGN WORK

Wendy Widmark of World Wide Widgets was so impressed with your suggestions on creating a Web site to advertise the company that she would like you to do an analysis of their competitor's Web sites. Knowing what you do about design, create a form you could fill out to use in evaluating other Web sites. In order for Ms. Widmark and others in the company to use the form, it must meet the following criteria:

- It should be divided into three parts: one for each kind of design—information design, interaction design, and presentation design.
- It should be easy to use and interpret.
- It should result in a letter grade or numeric score (or three scores if you choose—one for each type of design), which you can share with Ms. Widmark to give her an idea which of the company's competitor's Web sites are best.

WEB SITE

Designing with a Group

Meet with your design team and share your evaluation forms. Combine them into a single form that best fulfills the expectations listed above. Use your final form to evaluate two or three similar Web sites (on any topic). Discuss how the sites compare.

WRITING ABOUT TECHNOLOGY: Which Matters Most?

With what you know about Web site design to this point, write a 100-word answer, on a separate piece of paper, to the following question:

Based on what you have experienced and thought about while working in this chapter, which of the three elements of design do you consider to be the most important in the creation of a great Web site: information design, interaction design, or presentation design? Why?

_____

_____

_____

_____

_____

Information Design

Chapter Objectives

In this chapter you will explore the principles of information design as they pertain to Web sites. After reading Chapter 4, you will be able to:

1. identify and document your Web site's message.

2. identify and tailor your information for your Web site's audience.

3. identify and develop your Web site's purpose and scope.

4. structure your Web site's information into a flowchart.

The Parts of Information Design

The auditorium is filled with thousands of people, all there to hear you speak. Suddenly, the MC is introducing you; you are about to deliver a speech! In about three seconds, you will step up to the microphone and begin to speak. Then it dawns on you: What are you there to talk about? Who are these people, and why should they care what you have to say? Why are you giving this speech, anyway?

Sound far-fetched? Sound like a nightmare you've had? Well, it happens every day on the Web. Thousands of people visit Web sites looking for something interesting or important to them. Instead, they often find aimless, meaningless, disjointed, disorganized, and sometimes downright confusing information.

What is wrong with these Web sites?

There might be any number of reasons why a Web site fails. However, it is our experience that most Web sites fail because they neglect to answer three important questions before they develop their site:

- What is the message of this site?

- Who is the audience for this site?

- What is the purpose of this site?

These three questions help guide the information design process. By working with the principles of information design, you will make sure that your Web site avoids the mire of mediocrity. The answers to

Web Terms

design document

scope

random access structure

linear structure

hierarchical structure

mixed structure

chunks

flowchart

these three questions will guide your work and should be recorded into a **design document**.

Your design document will help you successfully develop your site. Just like a movie producer has a script that describes the words and actions of all the characters in a movie, the design document will be a guide to help you keep focused on the whys and wherefores of your Web site.

When you do information design you must consider what you want to say (the message), to whom you're going to say it (audience), and why you want to say it (purpose), among other things. As you look at these three fundamental aspects of information design, you probably notice that it is very hard to tell which one comes first—the audience, the message, or the purpose.

Here are some examples of how other Web site developers faced these three design issues with their topics:

- One bookseller's Web site exists to make money; therefore, making money (the purpose) is a primary consideration, followed closely by the books they are selling (the message), and the people to whom they are selling them (the audience).
- A student shared her university's sports history (the message) online. Those interested in the site included sports fans and alumni of the university (the audience). The site was used to help promote interest in the university's sports program (the purpose).
- Another Web site supports the families of people who suffer from Parkinson's disease. The audience (the families of Parkinson's disease sufferers) was planned first, then the purpose (to support the families with advice) and the message (in-depth information about Parkinson's disease and related medical research) was created.

As you can probably see by these examples, it is very hard to entirely separate these three design questions. You must consider and document all three issues in your design document. For instance, what if the bookseller's Web site concentrated so much on making money (the purpose) that it didn't display the books very well (the message), or didn't show respect for their customers (the audience)? Clearly, they wouldn't sell many books, they would lose customers, and the Web site's purpose—to make money—would be frustrated. Good design requires the careful consideration of all three issues.

Net Ethics — RESPECT the Web: The Simplicity Test

The Simplicity test has several levels. First, is your Web site easy to navigate? Can visitors find the information they need quickly and easily? If it is hard to find information, your visitors will become frustrated and may never come back your site again. Second, is the Web site easy to manage? Is your site organized in such a way that you can make changes and improvements quickly and easily? If there is a problem with one of your Web pages, can you find the page, make the correction, and repost the information quickly without corrupting links to other important information?

In Web site design, follow the KISSS principle. KISSS stands for "Keep It Simple, Simpler, Simplest!"

If you have taken the time to explain and document your site, you can make it easier for other Webmasters to make corrections in your absence. You may not be available a year from now when the site needs to be updated. If you have followed the KISSS principle and documented your site in a design document, you can make it easier for others to revisit your work and to make corrections. This shows respect for those that follow in your footsteps.

ACTIVITY

4.1

Objective:

In this activity you will learn to identify and document your Web site's message.

What Is My Web Site's Message?

As a Web page designer, your first task is often to identify and research your message. For example, when you write a term paper or business report, your first step is to brainstorm and select a general idea or the main topic that you're going to write about. After you have selected a topic, you must research it, learning all you can. Then you are ready to create a rough outline of what your are going to say. Later, you go back, review your research, and fill in your outline with more specifics and details. Only after you have organized all the information do you start writing.

A good way to decide what your Web site will be about is to brainstorm topics based on your own interests. That is exactly what this activity will have you do.

1. Brainstorm and write down ten topics in which you are interested. These can include hobbies, interests, pets, favorite school subjects, your family, work, or just about anything. If you are developing your site as a partnership or team, brainstorm ten topics with your team.

2. Copy the items in your list in the order in which they most interest you (or your team), with the most interesting topic first. (If you get stuck trying to decide which item should be first, compare them two at a time, putting a mark next to the one that wins each pairing. The one with the most marks is first, the one with the second most number of marks is second, and so forth.)

3. Examine the first topic in your prioritized list and ask yourself, "Can I create a great Web site based on this idea or topic?" If you don't feel you can build a Web site about your first topic, continue down the list until you have at least one topic that can make a great Web site. Your selection should be something that (1) you either know or are willing to learn about; (2) you are interested in; and (3) is not too narrow and not too broad.

4. Your topic of choice will become the message of your Web site. Consult with your instructor or team members on your message. Discuss its merits before you finally decide to develop your Web site around your chosen topic. Make sure it is a topic you will enjoy spending many hours working on.

5. Once you have consulted with your instructor on your message, open your word processor and complete your message statement beginning with the words, "*Message: This Web site will _____.*" This will be the beginning of your design document.

6. Spend some time (three to ten hours, outside of class) researching your message. Take your time and learn as much as you can. Naturally, the Web is a great resource to draw from. Make a short reference for each significant resource you find in your design document under the heading *Resource List.* Make a short note about

what each reference contains so you can remember it in the future. In Figure 4.1a below, a design document has been started for a university sports history site.

7 Save your design document with the file name *Design*.

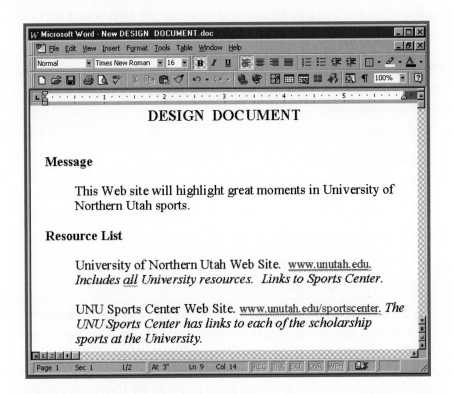

THINKING ABOUT TECHNOLOGY: WEB TOPICS

Some believe that the Web can be used to communicate any message at all. Can you think of any message that can't be communicated by way of the Web? Can you think of any that shouldn't be communicated through the Web?

Who Is My Web Site's Audience?

Once you have decided what your Web page is going to be about and have researched your topic, you will want to identify whom you want to have view and read your pages. This is called your *audience*. Your Web pages need to be tailored to meet the needs and expectations of your target audience.

An audience is a group of people who have something in common. Whatever it is they have in common should be somehow connected with the message of your Web site. Things that audiences can have in common include:

- Their age

- Where they live

- What they do for a living

- What style of clothes they like

- A language they speak

- Some kind of food they like

- A cause that they feel strongly about

To identify the audience for your Web site, you must identify what it is that the group has in common with your Web site. For example, it is not enough to say "the audience of my Web site are people who like fish." That might mean you are creating a site about tropical fish; in which case your audience will be those people who like to keep a particular type of fish as pets. It might also mean your site is about the best sushi in the world, in which case your audience might be anyone who likes to eat raw fish. Or it may even refer to people who like Phish—the rock group. In that case, your audience will be anyone who likes that group's music.

To identify your audience, you must not just say what they have in common, you must say what makes them unique or what makes them differ from other groups.

1. In your design document, write a description of your audience in a single paragraph. This is called an audience statement. Be specific enough that your audience will not be confused with any other group. The statement should be around 35 to 50 words long.

2. Insert your audience statement between your message statement and your resource list, as shown in Figure 4.2a. Your audience statement should state clearly what the audience has in common with your Web site's message. For instance, in Figure 4.2a the audience include fans of a university sports program. The description emphasizes currently enrolled students interested in such sports as basketball and yachting, but doesn't mention bowling and wrestling.

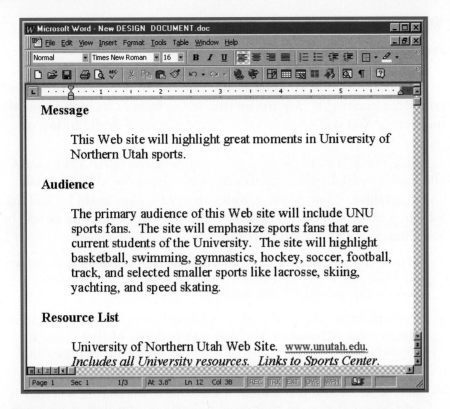

Figure 4.2a
Insert your audience statement
into your design document

Inside the Word window:

Message

This Web site will highlight great moments in University of
Northern Utah sports.

Audience

The primary audience of this Web site will include UNU
sports fans. The site will emphasize sports fans that are
current students of the University. The site will highlight
basketball, swimming, gymnastics, hockey, soccer, football,
track, and selected smaller sports like lacrosse, skiing,
yachting, and speed skating.

Resource List

University of Northern Utah Web Site. www.unutah.edu.
Includes all University resources. Links to Sports Center.

③ To make sure you've been thorough enough, share your audience
statement with a partner or classmate, and allow him or her to share
his or her own statement (if you are working in a team, do this within
your team). Discuss whether what you've written could be confused
with any other group or audience than the one you've identified.
Questions you and your partner or team may ask each other are:

- Does this audience statement include people who *wouldn't* be
  interested in this Web site?
- Why did you limit your audience?
- Are there other people who might want to look at this Web
  site that are *not* included in the audience statement?

Make corrections to your audience statement as needed and resave
your design document.

THINKING ABOUT TECHNOLOGY: SECONDARY AUDIENCES

Web sites often have secondary audiences, people for whom the site
was not intended, but who might also like it. In the example in Figure
4.2a, university fundraisers may wish to use the site to help raise money
for the school's sports program. Does your Web site have any
secondary audiences?

Design Desk
Who Is My Audience?

Here are some generalized
examples of a few Web page
audiences:
- People searching for other
  Web pages and information
  (examples: search engines
  like Excite and Web indexes
  like Yahoo!).
- People interested in your
  company, school, or organization (examples: company
  Web sites like Apple Computers' home page, school sites
  like Union High School's
  home page, or organization
  sites like the Web site for
  Future Business Leaders of
  America).
- People interested in a particular product, topic, or class
  (examples: software product
  Web sites like the Microsoft
  Office home page, a Web
  site for people who like cats,
  or a Web site for people
  taking an algebra class at
  your high school).
- Your instructor or employer
  (examples: a Web page you
  have to create for your class
  or a Web report you have to
  prepare for your company).
- Your friends and family
  (example: a personal Web
  page).
- You (example: a "bookmark"
  page that includes links to
  your favorite Web pages).

The audience is your most
important consideration when
you are designing your pages.

ACTIVITY
4.3

Objective:

In this activity, you will learn to identify and document your Web site's purpose as it relates to your audience and message.

What Is My Web Site's Purpose and Scope?

It is essential that you clarify the purpose of your Web site *before* you begin creating it. A purpose that is too broad can make your site ineffective. You will need to be very specific in your definition of purpose.

Using our fish example, let's say you have identified your target audience as people who like to eat sushi—Japanese-style raw fish and vegetables. What might a Web surfer who likes sushi be looking for when he or she comes across your site? Why would he or she be searching the Web for sites about sushi in the first place?

- Maybe the surfer is hungry and is looking for places that serve sushi in his or her town. In that case, a directory of sushi restaurants would fill the need.

- Perhaps he or she is planning to learn how to prepare sushi and wants some instruction on how that is done. In that case, an instructional Web site, one that teaches the skill of preparing sushi, is most appropriate.

- Maybe he or she just caught a fish and is wondering whether it can be eaten raw. In that case, a detailed information Web site about the types of fish that can be used for sushi is what is needed.

Notice that your Web site's content (message) and what you know about its audience can help you define your purpose. The more you know about what your audience knows and expects, the easier it is to craft a statement of purpose.

Design Desk *What Do They Already Know?*

If you don't have a basic understanding of what your audience already knows, you will tend to provide too much or too little information. For example, it would be silly for you to create a Web page whose audience included six-year-olds that included a sentence like, "A central problem in theoretical discourse is our lack of a common metatheoretical language and framework within which we can categorize and debate diverse positions" (W. R. Shadish. 1998. "Evaluation theory is who we are." American Journal of Evaluation. Memphis, Tennessee: JAI Press, Inc. p. 10). Most six-year-olds don't know enough to understand that sentence. (Taken out of context as it is, you probably don't either!)

Thinking about what your audience already knows will keep you from making these two common mistakes: talking over their heads and talking down to them. Talking over their heads is like that sentence in the preceding paragraph—they just won't understand it. Talking down to them means that you're telling them things they already know, making them lose interest in your Web site because they feel like you're showing off, or because they're just not learning anything. In either case, it probably won't meet their needs.

1 Conduct an audience analysis. If possible, interview members of your intended audience. (If you can't talk to representatives of your audience, you may need to make some educated guesses about them.) You could prepare a survey or interview potential members of your audience one on one. Ask them what they already know about your topic, and inquire what they expect to see in a Web site about your topic. Questions may include:

- What kind of information would cause you to visit a Web site on this topic?

- What do you already know about this topic?

- What do you want or need from a Web site on this topic?

- How would you like to see the information presented?

- What parts of the message are of greatest interest to you?

- What benefits could come from a Web site on this topic?

2 Write one or more paragraphs (at least 35 words) explaining the primary purpose of your site. Review your message and audience statements. Consider everything you learned while talking to your audience. Insert your purpose statement in your design document between your audience statement and your resource list. Be clear, concise, and direct in your purpose statement.

3 Write one or more paragraphs explaining what your audience already knows. This will be called the audience background statement. Insert this information after your purpose statement.

Once you have a pretty good idea of what your audience already knows, you can begin to talk about what your message will and won't cover—listing what you will and will not talk about on your Web site. This is called **scope**. Without a scope statement, it is easy to get caught up in your subject and write too much (or, without guidelines, you could write too little)! This can make it hard to finish your Web site on schedule. Detailing your scope will keep you focused on the important aspects of your topic.

4 Make two lists in your design document under the heading *Scope* (see Figure 4.3a on the next page). List three to five things that your site will present. Then make a list of three to five things that your site *won't* discuss. Use these two lists to help focus your later work and what it's limits are.

5 Share these additions to your design document with another user or your team. Have them evaluate whether they adequately explain what your audience knows and what the Web site should cover.

6 Rewrite your paragraphs as needed and save them to the design document you've been working on in the previous two activities.

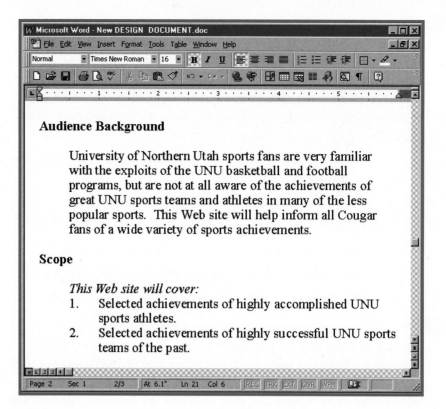

Figure 4.3a
Continue your design document by defining your project's purpose and scope and adding an audience background statement

THINKING ABOUT TECHNOLOGY: DESIGN DECISIONS

Can the definitions of your message, audience, purpose, background, and scope affect later decisions like what colors to use, what typeface to display, or what hyperlinks to include?

How Should the Message Be Structured?

ACTIVITY 4.4

Objective:
In this activity you will structure your Web site information into a flowchart.

To fulfill the purpose you've just outlined, your message must be organized in some way. Organization can come in many flavors, depending on what you are trying to accomplish. We need to take your message (the information on your Web site), and, based on what you know about your audience and purpose, organize it in preparation for content development and HTML and JavaScript coding.

Here are three sample organizational structures. Each has advantages and disadvantages that should mesh with your stated purpose.

Random Access Structure

One information structure is called **random access structure**. Random access lets you jump from one part of the site to another instantaneously. Random access sites are most appropriate when you want your user to have quick access to all the information all of the time, such as in a hobby site (see Figure 4.4a).

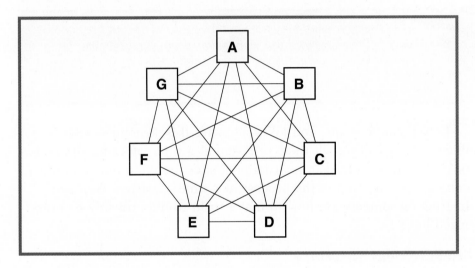

Figure 4.4a
Diagram of a random access site

Random access structure can be very confusing if the amount of information is large, but it is a good way to get everything out on the table, so to speak, so that your visitors can get to it easily.

For example, if there aren't too many places that sell sushi in your town, the random-access structure is probably a good way to organize your sushi restaurant directory so that your audience can move

SCOOP

Do you want to see an example of a random access site? Visit the Web page at *webdesign.swep.com*, Doorways to Design, and click on Door Number 6 to get a feel for this popular Web structure.

around it quickly. (If there are more than seven sushi restaurants, a hierarchical Web site might be a better choice; see below.)

Linear Structure

Another type of organization is **linear structure**. A linear organization works best when you want your user to see one page at a time and then move on, like reading a book or explaining a step-by-step process. Linear structure is used when you don't want to give away the end of your story before you have finished it! Figure 4.4b shows a diagram of linear structure.

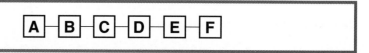

Figure 4.4b
Diagram of a linear site

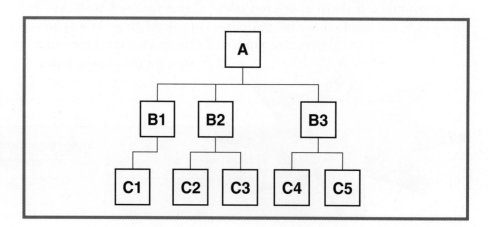

Linear sites may not sound very exciting, but they can be very informative. Visit the *webdesign.swep.com* Web site, go to Doorways to Design, and click Door Number 7 to see what we mean.

Books, comic strips, and jokes all share this structure—they are linear: You step through them one step at a time, often for dramatic or humorous effect. Also, instructional sites are often linear so they can explain one step of the process at a time. Clearly a Web site instructing someone on how to make sushi would probably be organized linearly.

Hierarchical Structure

Another very common structure is the **hierarchical structure**. Basically, a hierarchy looks like a family tree with parents and children (and sometimes grandchildren), like in Figure 4.4c.

```
                    A
        ┌───────────┼───────────┐
       B1          B2          B3
     ┌──┴──┐     ┌──┴──┐
    C1    C2    C3    C4    C5
```

Figure 4.4c
Diagram of a hierarchy

Door Number 8 on the *webdesign.swep.com* Web site will let you see a classic site using a hierarchical strategy. This is one of the most popular Web site structures.

Hierarchies are a good way to organize informational sites. Using categories and subcategories—something like your English teacher taught you to do with an outline—by determining categories, then subcategories, and so forth.

Our university sports history site might be organized as a hierarchy, with the top category introducing the site and linking to pages about each individual sport. From the individual sports pages, links could be created to stories about the achievements of the teams and individuals in those sports.

Mixed Structure

Unfortunately, information does not always fit into such neat, clean structures. With some sites, some of your information should be organized one way and some in another. Sometimes you need a site that is partly random access, somewhat linear, and at times hierarchical, as shown in Figure 4.4d. This is know as a mixed structure.

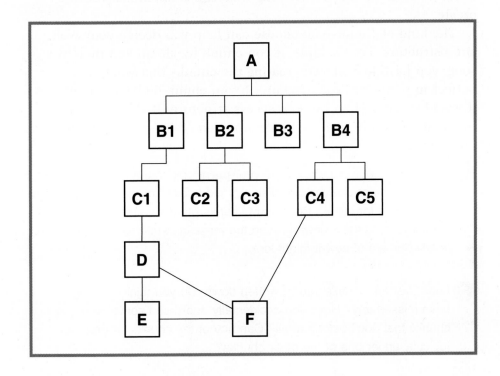

Figure 4.4d
A mixed structure

Most sites use a variety of structures. Got to *webdesign.swep.com*, Doorways to Design, and select Door Number 9 to see a great example of a mixed Web site structure.

Organizing Your Message

To turn your message into any structure, you must first break your message up into smaller pieces of information we call **chunks**. This breaking of information into chunks will give you the building blocks of your structure—what you're going to put in those little boxes on your diagram.

Let's use another of our fish (or rather, Phish) examples. Suppose you were creating a Web site for fans of the rock group Phish. One way you could break up the information on your site would be by album or CD titles. Each album would be a chunk. Then, you could break up each album by the songs that were on it. The songs become a second level of chunking. Or, let's say that your Web site's audience is going to be most interested in the members of the band. In this case the members' names form the chunks of information. Another way you might break up the information is by date, making a history of the band. In any case, the idea is to break the message up into the parts of which it is made. Remember, the purpose of breaking this information up is to make it fill your audience's needs—that is the key to deciding what kinds of chunks you will create.

The kind of chunks you choose can help you decide your Web site's structure. For example, if you chunk by album and then by song, you have just started creating the chunks that would be perfect in a hierarchical structure. If you chunk by band members, it would fit nicely in a random access structure. If you chunked the information into historical chunks, they could be structured linearly into a history.

1. On a fresh piece of paper, write your main topic in the middle of the paper, like: "university sports history," "old books," or "what kinds of fish can be used for sushi." Brainstorm chunks of information related to this topic and write them down around the message statement. Figure 4.4e is an example of how it might look.

2. Look over the chunks you've written down. Do you think you might have missed any? Have you accidentally duplicated some? Are there chunks that don't belong at all? Can any of the chunks be grouped topically under one of the other chunks?

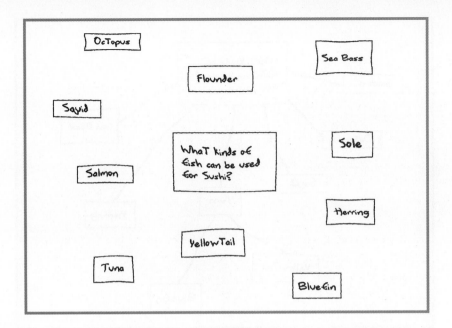

Figure 4.4e
Brainstormed site with chunked
information

3 On your paper, draw a line from each chunk to the message statement,
or if a chunk is more closely related to another chunk, draw a line
between them (see Figure 4.4f).

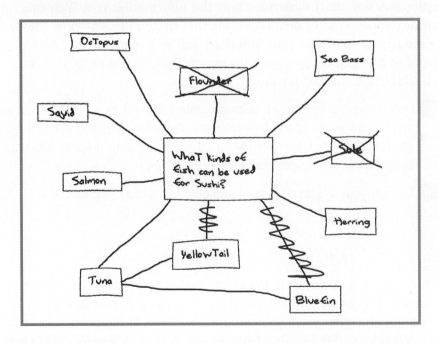

Figure 4.4f
A sample of a site's chunks,
with lines drawn (and some
crossed out)

4 Look carefully at your paper. Some kind of structure should begin to
emerge. (You may need to cross out some of the lines you have drawn,
and draw others to make the structure clear.)

5 Redraw your chart, being careful to note how things are
related so you can draw it more neatly. Draw boxes around the chunks
and lines between the boxes to show relationships. You may need to
repeat this exercise a few times before the chart is clear like the one in
Figure 4.4g. Review the different structures we discussed above if
you're not clear on how to organize your chunks.

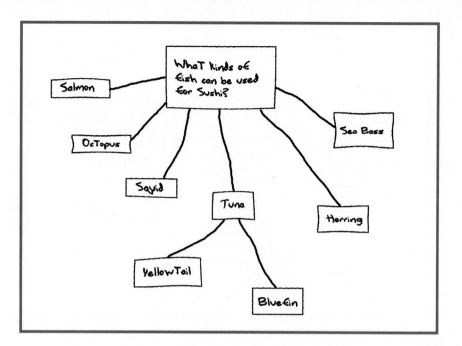

Figure 4.4g
Chunked information arranged
in a hierarchical structure

What you have just finished is called a **flowchart**. (Notice that the flowchart in the illustration is the beginning of a hierarchical organization.) A flowchart illustrates how the information in a Web site (or any other kind of document, for that matter) flows—how they relate to one another. Your flowchart will help you see and understand at one glance how your information is put together. It is a valuable addition to your design document.

6 Use drawing software and re-create your flowchart as a picture or as a graphic using one of the four Web site structures identified in this chapter: random, linear, hierarchical, or mixed. Insert your diagram into your design document under the heading *Flowchart.*

7 Resave your design document and print out a copy. Nice work!

THINKING ABOUT TECHNOLOGY: FLOWCHARTS

A flowchart is a snapshot of the information on your Web site, that is, it shows at a glance how the information on you site is organized. Are there any other ways you can use flowcharts to represent information. What kind of flowchart might you use to show a "snapshot" of your audience? Of your purpose?

WEB VOCABULARY

Define the following terms:

1. design document
2. scope
3. random access structure
4. linear structure
5. hierarchical structure
6. mixed structure
7. chunks
8. flowchart

WEB REVIEW

Give a short answer to the following questions, giving specific examples in each:

1. What kind of Web sites would benefit from a random access structure?

_____

_____

_____

_____

2. What kind of Web sites would benefit from a linear structure?

_____

_____

_____

_____

3. What kind of Web sites would benefit from a hierarchical structure?

_____

_____

_____

_____

4. What kind of Web sites would benefit from a mixed structure?

_____

_____

_____

_____

WEB SITE UNDER CONSTRUCTION

Wally Woodword owns a small cabinet making business. He creates kitchen and bathroom cabinets and custom wood furnishings for homes. His buyers are homeowners. He uses a variety of woods for his projects. including oak, pine, birch, maple, poplar, and cherry. He wants to sell more cabinets.

Wally feels that if he can create a Web site, he can reach more homeowners. He has asked you to come up with the information design for his new site. Create a short design document for his site. Be creative! If you can impress Wally with your ideas, you may get the job of designing his Web site. Include the following elements:

- Message statement
- Audience statement
- Purpose statement
- Audience background statement
- Scope
  - This Web site will cover . . .
  - This Web site will not cover . . .
- Flowchart

WEB SITE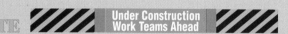

Wally Woodword's Wood Works, Inc., faces a great deal of competition. Wally is wondering several things:
1. What other cabinet makers have Web sites?
2. What online resources are available about cabinet making?
3. What information is available about various kinds of wood used in woodworking (oak, pine, birch, maple, poplar, cherry)?

Wally wants a resource list that includes resources on each of these topics. Searching all of this information on the Web might be difficult for one person, but if you divide up the task between three or more team members, it will be a snap!

As a team, prepare a research list for Wally on each of these three topics.

WRITING ABOUT TECHNOLOGY: Design

Having created two design documents, you now understand a great deal about the basics of information design. You have learned how to define the audience, purpose, and the message of a Web site. With what you know about design to this point, write a 100-word answer to one of the three inquiries that follow:

Option 1. Based on what you have learned so far, which element of information design do you feel is the most important to define: the audience, the purpose, or the message? Explain your answer.

Option 2. Explain how the three elements of audience, purpose, and message work together to help organize a great Web site.

Option 3. Why is it helpful to define the scope of your Web site?

Interaction Design

Chapter Objectives:

In this chapter, you will learn and apply the principles of interaction design. After reading Chapter 5, you will be able to:

1. create a storyboard that represents the interactions of your Web site.

2. identify the welcome page of your Web site.

3. show your visitors where they are while navigating your site.

4. decide how your visitors will move around your site.

5. use context devices to organize the user interface for your Web site.

Web Terms

storyboard

title page

welcome page

context device

banner

table of contents

place finding

The Three Elements of Interaction Design

Interaction design is concerned with how visitors move around and interact with your Web site. As a designer you will need to concern yourself with how the information will be organized on the pages (organization), how people will find their way around your Web site (navigation), and what controls you give your users to work with (interactivity).

As you continue planning your Web site, you will need to plan in careful detail how to organize your pages so that your audience can navigate the site and learn your message with a minimum of hassle. Interactivity, or participation, helps bring your message home to the audience. If your Web site visitors are participating in some way, they are more likely to remember what you have to say.

Internet portal sites like go.com, snap.com, yahoo.com, and excite.com can be used to find examples of navigation systems, context devices, and other user interface techniques. Search for the sites of businesses you admire or universities you think may have a great Web site. Observe how they solved their navigation problems and record these examples in your design document.

Objective:

In this activity you will create a storyboard to represent the interactions of your Web site.

Tinker Toys for Designers: The Storyboard

Sometimes engineers create models to decide whether something they are trying to build is going to work. This gives them the opportunity to visualize and to test a scale model before they build the life-sized item.

Web designers have a similar tool called a **storyboard**. It is based on a technique developed by Walt Disney to help make animated cartoons. Animators aren't the only ones who use storyboards to plan things. A storyboard is a perfect tool for planning a Web site.

Making a storyboard is very simple. It's made up of cards or pieces of paper on which you write ideas. These cards can then be organized, moved about, added to, or taken away until you are comfortable with how they are arranged. You can use the cards to represent individual Web pages or structural parts of a single Web page.

HOT TIP

Storyboards are often arranged on corkboards using pins or tacks, or they are placed on magnetic boards with magnets to make them easy to move around as needed. Storyboarding software is also available.

1. Find a number of blank 3x5 index cards, or cut pieces of blank paper to approximately the same size.

2. Open your design document and turn to the flowchart you created in Activity 4.4.

3. Each box on your flowchart should have a name or a title written inside that represents a chunk of information that you have defined (see Figure 4.4g in Chapter 4). Copy the words from the boxes on your flowchart to the top of your 3x5 cards. Use one card for each box on your flowchart. Leave plenty of room on the cards—you'll be writing lots more on them.

4. Arrange the 3x5 cards on a piece of poster board, a white board, or on a blank wall using small pieces of tape on the back of each card to hold them in place. Start by arranging them in the same pattern as the topics or "chunks" of information appearing on your flowchart. Don't paste them in place yet—you need to be able to move them around.

THINKING ABOUT TECHNOLOGY: USING STORYBOARDS

Could you use a storyboard to plan a speech you are giving? How about a party? What other kinds of activities could you plan using a storyboard?

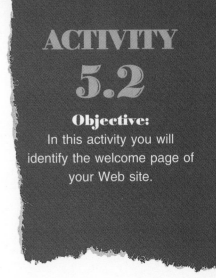

ACTIVITY
5.2

Objective:
In this activity you will identify the welcome page of your Web site.

Start at the Beginning

The front page of every newspaper (and a lot of Web sites) has a **banner** that stretches across the top, identifying the paper. Famous banners like the *Wall Street Journal* and the *New York Times* are classic examples. Similarly, books have **title pages** that tell you the title of the book, the author, and the publisher. Television programs have opening titles that tell you the name of the show. Banners, title pages, and opening credits (sometimes known as starting devices) provide signals to you that you're looking at the beginning of something—at the starting point. Web pages are no different.

For a Web site, the starting point is a **welcome page**—what the Web page visitors see first when they find your Web site. This is also known as the index page or the home page. From here they will navigate to the rest of your Web site.

As you examined the different kinds of structures from Chapter 4, did you notice that some of them have a natural starting point? In the case of a linear structure, it's the one on the left—the "first page" (See Figure 5.2a).

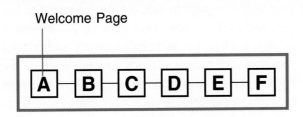

Figure 5.2a
The first page in a linear Web site will be the welcome page

In the hierarchical structure, it's the single box at the top (see Figure 5.2b.)

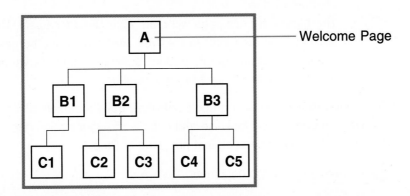

Figure 5.2b
The top page in a hierarchical Web site will be the welcome page

In the random access structure, any page can be the starting point because all the pages lead to all the others. But usually, there's one that can be moved to the "center" of things and can be designated as the starting point (see Figure 5.2c).

Welcome Page

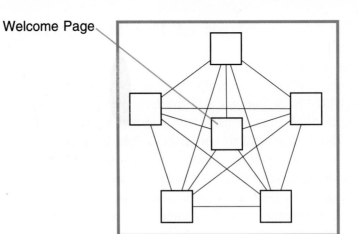

Figure 5.2c
The center page in a random access Web site will become the welcome page

1. Identify your welcome page. Which card do you think would make the best starting point for your Web site visitors? Write "WP" (for welcome page) in the top right corner of the card that will represent your starting point on your storyboard. (In some structures—like random access—you may need to create and add a new card as your welcome page.)

2. Start designing your welcome page. Pull your welcome page card (with the WP) from your storyboard and start sketching a rough outline what you want your welcome page to look like. Use a pencil so you can sketch, erase, and sketch again. Make sure the title of your site is written at or near the top. The title can become your banner if you plan it as such. Plan how your banner will look on your welcome page. Will it be all text or will it include a graphic or an image with multimedia effects? If you make a mistake or change your mind, create a new card.

3. Place your welcome page back on your storyboard.

4. Open your design document and write the heading *Welcome Page* and add a one-paragraph description (about 75 words) as to the purpose and content of this important page. The following is an example.
   Welcome Page
   The banner for this page will read, *Fish Used for Sushi*. The page will welcome the visitor to the Web site, explain the purpose of the site in a short paragraph, and list several links to the various kinds of fish that can be used to prepare sushi.

5. If you are talented with graphic software, draw a sample of what your welcome page may look like and copy it into your design document under the description you just prepared in Step 3.

6. Resave your design document.

THINKING ABOUT TECHNOLOGY: STARTING DEVICES

What is the starting device for a movie? What is the starting device for a magazine? What is the starting device for a class period or a business meeting? What is the starting device for a trial in a court of law?

Organizing Your Pages into a Uniform Context

ACTIVITY 5.3

Objective:
In this activity you will learn to use context devices to organize the user interface for your Web site.

Can you tell when a television commercial is coming on? Why is that? TV broadcast stations use signals, called **context devices**, to tell you that a commercial is coming. Sometimes they cut or fade to a black screen. Then there is often a short title sequence. You may not even noticed these devices, but without them, you might start to confuse the program with the commercials (something the sponsors would probably love, but the television producers would not).

Newspapers, books, and magazines also use context devices to help you tell where you are and where to go next. Headings, headlines, page numbers, and columns guide you through printed documents and help you understand the context of what you are reading.

There are some obvious context devices on Web pages, too. Context devices include:

- A **banner** to tell users what the page is about (like the headline in a newspaper)

- A heading, or several headings to describe portions of the content (like chapter titles and subheadings in a book)

- Content in the form of pictures and text (like the pictures in a magazine or next to a story in the newspaper)

- Pictures, texts, or backgrounds that tell users what Web site this Web page is part of. This type of context device can be subtle and understated. It is usually how the page looks, but can include a graphic that can be found on each page.

- Navigation bars that appear on each page on the Web site.

1 Look at Figure 5.3a. Can you identify all of the possible context devices on this page? Name three of them on a separate sheet of paper:

1. _____

2. _____

3. _____

Motion Capture

Planning and executing the movements of objects can often be accomplished through the use of motion capture. In a recent animated full-feature film, actors were hooked up to electrodes connected to computers. They were then asked to act like certain characters in the animated movie. The movements were then recorded in the computer, where programmers and multimedia artists took over, who animated the characters by matching their movements' to the real actors' movements and created the storyboard for the entire film. The use of actors as "mimes" saved a great deal of time in the development process and gave the animated characters more lifelike movements.

The Web and television will soon use a lot of the same kind of motion-capture technologies. How might the techniques used in the creation of animated films help create more exciting and animated Web pages?

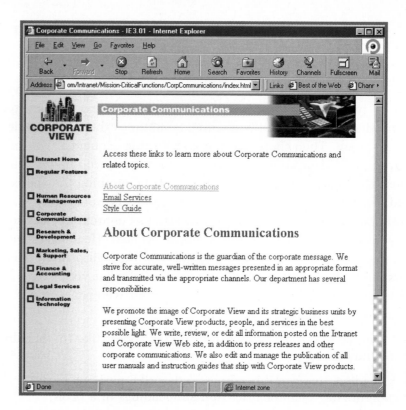

Figure 5.3a
A Corporate View Web corporate communications page using several context devices (jump to page 81 and read the Scoop to see if your answers are correct)

2 From your storyboard select a page other than the welcome page. We will call this a content card. All the cards on your storyboard except for your welcome page card are considered content cards.

3 On a new content card, sketch out a rough idea of what you think this page should look like. Block out squares where you intend to display text, and make sketches where you are going to place graphics. Then, on the same card, define two context devices. One can be a picture found on each page. Another can be a consistent color on each Web page site. One can be a "Return to Welcome Page" button or a navigation bar that can be found on every page. Don't be too fastidious about how it looks. This is just a rough sketch, not a finished product, so if it takes you more than about ten minutes to create this first card, it's too detailed.

4 Create two additional variations of the same page. Take three more index cards to create at least three more drawings, each a variation of your page ideas. Organize the content differently on each card.

5 Share your three sketches with a partner (if you're a member of a design team, share them with your team). With their help, decide which of the sketches is the best one for your content. Place the winning card back on your storyboard.

6 Each of your cards, which will later be developed into Web pages, requires the same context devices. Quickly sketch your context devices on each of the cards on your storyboard.

7 Open your design document and defend your choice from Step 5. Why did you choose the context and navigation aids you sketched in this activity? Enter the words *Context Devices* and write a short paragraph (under 100 words) describing the context and navigation devices you have selected and why you find them effective.

Context Devices

I chose a navigation bar, a common background color scheme, and links back to the welcome page as my navigation and context devices because . . .

8 If you are talented with graphics software, draw a sample of what your context devices may look like and copy it into your design document under the description you just wrote in Step 7.

9 Resave your design document.

THINKING ABOUT TECHNOLOGY: DOWN THE ROAD

Are there any context devices that help people as they drive down the road and navigate through traffic jams? What technologies have been created to create a safe context for motorists? How do these devices help prevent accidents?

Design Desk *What Is a Metaphor Like?*

A metaphor uses examples in the real world to help designers organize their work. For example, airlines may use a graphic of a check-in desk at an airport to guide Web site visitors through the process of ordering airline tickets online. Good metaphors are hard to create. Here are some ideas to help stretch your metaphor muscles:

Suppose you are creating a site that has the theme of exploration. What ideas or metaphors might you use to give the feeling of exploration? Here are some ideas: compass, astrolabe, ships, maps, ocean waves. Or you might choose space exploration: astronauts, space shuttles, planets, maybe even lasers and aliens. What metaphors about exploration would your audience relate to? How might these be used? What do you think a button with a picture of a compass on it does? How about a button with a laser on it?

When you add navigation and structure to a metaphor, your site will really begin to take off. A strong metaphor can make your site very powerful.

SCOOP

On page 79 you were asked to identify the context devices on a Web page. There are five. A color bar on the left side of the window places the same color on all similar Web pages. Inside that color bar is a list of links that are consistent throughout the site. The Corporate Communication banner appears on to top of every page in the section. The Corporate View logo in the top left corner also appears on all pages and is hyperlinked back to the welcome page. Finally, the hypertext links help visitors access other important parts of this site.

ACTIVITY

5.4

Objective:
At the end of this activity you will learn ways to help your visitor move around or navigate your site.

Now Where Do We Go?

"Would you tell me, please, which way I ought to walk from here?"

"That depends a good deal on where you want to get to," said the Cat.

"I don't much care where—" said Alice.

"Then it doesn't much matter which way you walk," said the Cat.

"—so long as I get somewhere," Alice added as an explanation.

"Oh, you're sure to do that," said the Cat, "if you only walk long enough."

When you are in an unfamiliar building, like a museum, library, or large shopping mall, you will often find a large map containing the words "You Are Here" pointing to a spot on the map, like Figure 5.4a. This map provides you with the two elements of good navigation: It tells you how to get around and tells you where you are right now in relation to the whole.

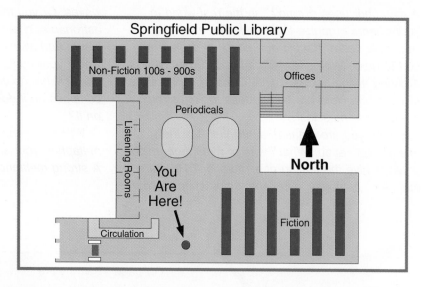

Figure 5.4a
A typical building map

That is what good navigation in a Web site should do. It should show you

• where you can go

• where you are right now

If you think about it, you'll see that these two are closely related. How can you tell where you want to go if you don't know where you are right now?

Where Are You Going?

Web browser buttons along the top of the browser help make Web page navigation easy. They allow your audience to "back out" of a page or to "go home" to where they started from if they get lost. However, the surest sign of amateur design is if the visitors get lost in the Web site and need to use the "back" or "home" buttons to get unlost. There are many ways that a visitor may navigate and interact with your site, and it starts on your welcome page.

A welcome page can be like a title page, or it can be like a **table of contents**. A title page explains what the site is about and displays banners and pictures that will attract visitors to delve deeper into your Web site. A table of contents is simply a list of places your visitor can go. Like a table of contents in a book, you can move directly to the page by clicking on the link.

We recommend that your welcoming page combine both: a title page *and* a table of contents. From here you can include:

- a list of links to the other pages

- hyperlinked pictures scattered on the page

- a navigation bar with buttons to the most popular parts of your site

- clickable areas (text, graphics, or buttons) to take users elsewhere, usually to navigate the site

After you have decided how your users will move from your welcome page to your content pages, you need to find a way to allow them to move back to the starting point or to move them ahead to other Web pages. There are many ways to do this, including the use of the following elements:

- A button or link as away to get back to the welcome page.

- Hypertext links allow visitors to jump around a Web site. They look different from the rest of the text by appearing underlined and in a different color, usually in blue or purple.

- A navigation bar with buttons to the most popular parts of your site, including the welcome page.

Some welcome pages have several of these elements! This welcome page by Candesa Corporation in Figure 5.4b has a simple navigation bar and a sidebar list of links.

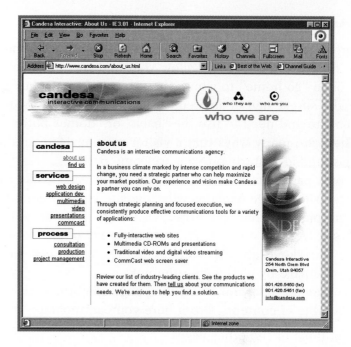

Figure 5.4b
The Candesa Web page has a
three-item navigation bar and a
sidebar list

Linear structures often don't have a menu or table of contents (though, like a book, they can). In a linear structure, the navigation control it is often three simple buttons: one to take you to the next Web page, one to take you back to the previous Web page, and one to take you to the welcome page, each in a single click (see Figure 5.4c).

Figure 5.4c
Navigation controls for a linear
structure

1 Go to Door Number 10 on the *webdesign.swep.com* Web site, Doorways to Design. Look at the welcoming Web page that comes up. On a piece of paper, answer these questions:
- What things make it clear that this is a welcoming Web page?
- Can you tell what the entire site is going to be about?
- What clues have they given you to help you decide where to go next?
- Which of these navigation elements could you use in your welcome page?

2 Select Door Number 11 and analyze the site that appears. Answer these questions about this site:
- How do you know that this is a welcome page?
- Can you tell what the entire site is going to be about?
- What clues have they given you to help you decide where to go next?
- Which of these navigation elements could you use in your welcome page?

3 Given the structure and content of your site, select a navigation method that you would like to use. You can use a navigation bar, a table of contents, or hyperlinks. On your welcome page card sketch the method you will use to move your visitors from your welcome page to other information content or Web pages on the site. Remember, you can use a new card to redraw the welcome page if you need to.

4 Given the structure and content of your site, select a method to get from your content pages back to your welcome page and elsewhere on your site. In a linear structure or random access structure, this may be a single button or link. In a hierarchical structure it may involve steps to navigate back up the hierarchy to the home page. Write or sketch the method you select on each card on your storyboard. If you decide to use a button bar, define each button and explain where each button will take your visitor.

5 Share your navigation methods with a partner, or, if you are working as a team, with your team members. Discuss whether the methods chosen for navigation are best suited to your Web site, and make changes as necessary.

6 When you have finalized both methods (how to move from your welcome page and how to move back) add these methods to all of your content cards. Remember, you can use new cards to redraw cards if you need to.

7 Open your design document and explain your navigation system. Why did you choose the navigation aids you sketched in this activity? Enter the words *Navigation and Interaction* and write a short paragraph (under 100 words) describing the context and navigation devices you have selected and why you find them effective.

> *Navigation and Interaction*
>
> I chose a navigation bar, which serves as both a context device and as an interactive navigation tool. I also have a picture that will appear on each page that, if clicked on, will take the visitor back to my welcome page. Interactivity is enhanced by . . .

8 If you are skilled with graphics software, draw a sample of what your navigation tools may look like and copy them into your design document under the description you just prepared in Step 7.

9 Resave your design document.

THINKING ABOUT TECHNOLOGY: AUDIENCE AND PURPOSE

Go back and read the message, audience, scope, and purpose statements you wrote in Chapter 4. Which navigation system will best meet your audience's needs? Could your navigation system be improved to communicate more clearly your message to your audience with your purpose?

Design Desk
Questions, Questions

In Chapter 4 you identified several questions that helped you create the initial design document. Here are some questions to help you with this chapter:

- *How would it be best to show your user the way?*
- *How will they find their way around the site? How will they know where they are in the structure of the site?*
- *Is there a graphic or metaphor that would help them understand the information in the site better?*
- *How can I make the site easier or more fun to use?*

ACTIVITY
5.5

Objective:
At the end of this activity you will learn ways to let your visitors know where they are on your Web site.

Knowing Where You Are

Now that your visitors know how to find their ways from one place to the next, you need to give them clues as to where they are right now. This is sometimes called **place finding**. Techniques for place finding in your Web site also differ depending on the structure of the site. In a story or other linear structure, you may have a page number on each page. Having the page number prominently displayed, like Figure 5.5a, will help your viewer know where they are.

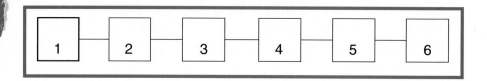

Figure 5.5a
A Web page with a page number

You can also add the total number of pages like this: "page 3 of 12." That not only tells visitors where they are (page 3), it tells them where the are in relation to the whole story or sequence of pages (about a fourth of the way through). See Figure 5.5b for an example.

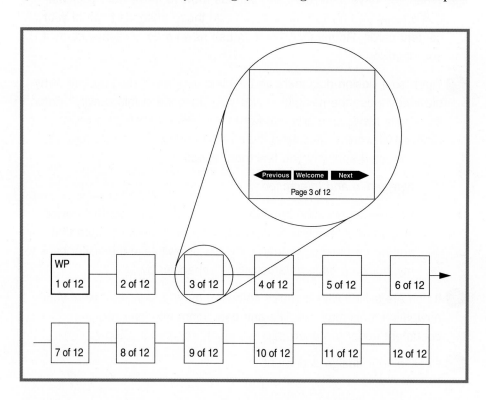

Figure 5.5b
A Web page with a page number in the form "page x of y"

In a random access structure, it is a little more difficult, since you can basically get from anywhere to anywhere. In this case, a simple page title is usually enough, providing that the links to the other pages use the same titles (see Figure 5.5c). You could also use an illustration, picture, or graphical icon.

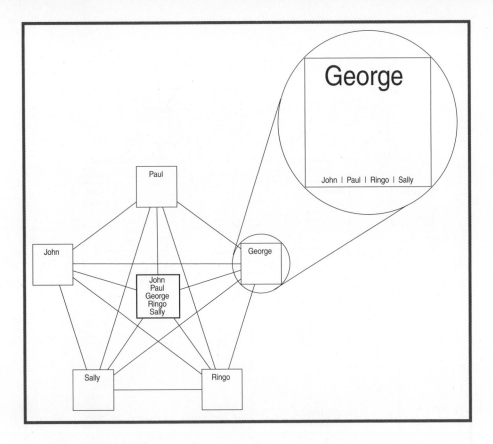

Figure 5.5c
A random access Web page with titles

One of the most common Web structures is hierarchical structure. It can also be one of the most complicated to illustrate. However, a simple method called "path" has been developed to show the viewers where they are. Figure 5.5d shows how the movement down a hierarchy is translated into a path. In this case, the user has navigated from the "Animals" page through the "Horses" and "Racehorses" categories to a page about "Standard-bred" horses. A common way to show this is to separate the items in the path with some kind of punctuation (in this case, a line break, some spaces, and an arrow) to show what path was traveled to get where the user is now.

1 Given the structure and content of your site, select a method to use to show your viewer where he or she is in your Web site. You may use one of the techniques above or make up your own. Sketch your ideas on your content cards for future reference.

2 Share your ideas for place finding with a partner or with your team. Make corrections to your idea as necessary.

3 Sketch the basics of your place-finding method onto all your cards. Remember, you can redraw and replace cards on your storyboard if you need to.

4 Write a brief description of how your are going to help visitors through place finding. Add this description in your design document. Enter the words *Place Finding* and write a short paragraph (under 100 words) describing your place-finding strategy. Draw a picture of your solution and include it in your design document under your paragraph.

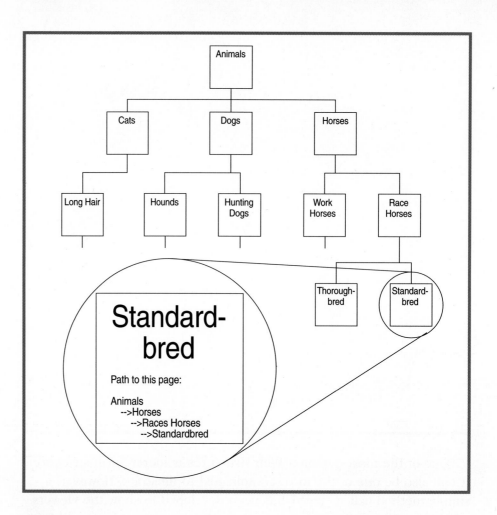

Figure 5.5d
The path from the general term "Animals" to the specific term "Standard-bred" race horses

⑤ Resave your design document.

THINKING ABOUT TECHNOLOGY: ON THE ROAD AGAIN

Once again, out on the open road in your car, are there any place-finding devices that can help you find your way? Especially in construction zones, are there any technologies that help the motorist make decisions about where they are and where they need to go?

Net Ethics   RESPECT the Web: The Purpose Test

As we have discussed earlier, every Web page should have a purpose, that is, it should make a point of some kind. Your purpose may be to sell a product or to talk about your favorite things. It may be to comment on the latest crisis in the Middle East. There are many ways to get your point across—with words, graphics, pictures, sounds, and even video. Whatever your purpose, make sure your page gets the main point across to the reader or viewer of your page and that unintended messages don't appear.

- If a page has no beneficial *purpose*, what should you do with the page?
- If the *purpose* you have defined is inappropriate, what should you do with the page?
- If the page has a double meaning that you had not considered previously, what should you do with the page?

These are questions only you can answer. Sometimes, your purpose in developing a page may be perceived differently by others. It may be well to ask them, "I had this purpose in mind. Do you think this Web page gets my point across successfully to the audience?"

WEB VOCABULARY

Define the following terms:

1. storyboard

2. title page

3. welcome page

4. context device

5. banner

6. table of contents

7. place finding

WEB REVIEW

Give a short answer to the following questions:

1. Why are storyboards such a powerful tool in Web page design?

2. What is the purpose of a banner and why are they used frequently on Web sites?

3. Why are welcome pages needed; in other words, what purposes do they serve?

4. What is a context device? Explain these powerful tools with examples.

WEB SITE STORYBOARD

Continuing to advise *Wally Woodword's Wood Works, Inc* develop their Web site, you are asked to story-board the cabinetmaker's Web site. (Review the Net Project in Chapter 4.) Storyboard the site based on what you know about:

- welcome pages
- banners
- context devices
- navigation systems
- place finders

Enter your new design ideas for Wally in the design document you started creating for the cabinet maker in Chapter 4.

WEB SITE — Under Construction Work Teams Ahead

Form a team of three or four people and search the Web looking for the best examples you can find of the following:

- best welcome page
- best banner
- best navigation system
- best place-finding idea
- most impressive context devices

Prepare a short presentation concerning each of your five selections. Present your choices to the other teams and explain why you selected the pages you did.

WRITING ABOUT TECHNOLOGY Navigation and Place Finding

With what you have learned about interaction design to this point, write a 100-word response to one of the following:

Option 1:   What is the most useful navigation system that you have seen? Why do you prefer this system over the other possible options.

Option 2:   Are place-finding techniques really important? Explain your answer and include samples of good place-finding techniques you have seen in your searching of the Web.

_____

_____

_____

_____

_____

_____

CHapter 6

Presentation Design

Chapter Objectives:

In this chapter, you will plan the visual design of your Web pages. After reading Chapter 6 you will be able to:

1. use thumbnail sketches and art roughs to plan your visual design.

2. identify various possible themes for your Web site.

3. plan background, foreground, and other design elements.

4. apply a theme and related design elements to your Web site.

5. use a grid to organize design elements including proportion, balance, unity, and space.

Web Terms

thumbnail sketches

greeking

rough sketch

visual theme

tiled

grid

unity

balance

proportion

Visualizing Your Web Site

Presentation design is sometimes called visual design. It is planning how your Web site will look:

- What colors will look good together on your site?

- What fonts or styles of type you will use for the written part of your Web pages?

- What graphics and multimedia effects are needed?

- How will all of these elements be combined or arranged into an attractive layout?

There have been many books written on the subject of graphic or presentation design. In fact, when you say the word *design* or *designer*, most people think you are speaking of graphic design or a graphic designer. What follows are some tips and techniques that will help you design your Web site in an organized way.

Graphic Designers

It's probably pretty obvious that the more you know about creating art, the better you will be a making your site look good. But you may be surprised to learn that the people who have the most to do with creating a "look" for a Web site are not artists—at least not in the traditional sense. These are not necessarily people who know how to paint or draw (though many have those talents as well). Rather, these are people who know how to put things together to make them look visually appealing. That is why they are called graphic designers, not graphic artists.

ACTIVITY 6.1

Objective:

In this lesson, you will learn to create thumbnails and rough sketches as tools in presentation design.

Thumbnails and Rough Sketches

Professional Web designers doodle. These little drawings help them think about the visual aspects of the Web pages they are designing. They make lots of drawings before deciding on an idea. You can also use sketches to help make choices about your Web site's presentation design.

The little drawings that graphic designers make are called **thumbnail sketches** because they are rough and very small (like your thumbnail—though they're not really *that* small). These thumbnail sketches are similar to the sketches you made in the last chapter for your storyboard, but they serve a different purpose. A storyboard helps you get a handle on your Web site's interaction; thumbnails help you focus on how your Web pages will look.

One way to get rid of some of the detail is to use **greeking**, which is substituting straight or squiggly lines for text. Though you will probably want to go ahead and write out the headings, you can use heavier lines for larger or bold text, and lighter lines for smaller or lighter text. Greeking can give you the "look" of text in your thumbnail sketch without taking the time to write it all out. Figure 6.1a is a thumbnail sketch of the Web page illustrated in Figure 6.1b.

Figure 6.1a
A thumbnail sketch of the University of Minnesota Web page

HOT TIP
Thumbnail Hints

A typical size for a thumbnail is a couple of inches wide by an inch or so tall, though they can be larger if need be. One of the tricks to making thumbnails is that you don't spend a lot of time on them. Do them quickly. If you don't like your thumbnail, draw another one. Creating thumbnails is like brainstorming for Web page designers.
If you can't complete a thumbnail in about 30 seconds, you're spending too much time on it.

Figure 6.1b
The actual Web page for the University of Minnesota

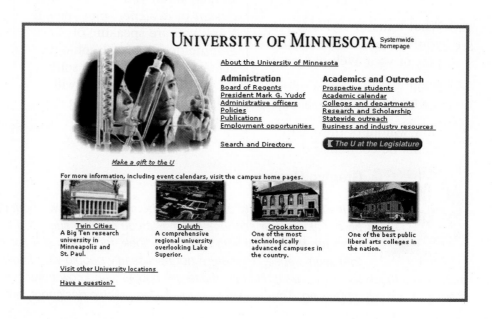

Now it's your turn.

1 For this activity you will need to pick six Web pages that you like. Search the Web. Choose pages that aren't all the same—ones that have lots of variety on them so they'll be fun to make thumbnails of. List your six choices here by listing their titles and their URLs as shown in the sample number 0.

	Name of Site	URL or Web Address
0.	South-Western Educational Publishing	www.swep.com
1.		
2.		
3.		
4.		
5.		
6.		

2 Fold a blank sheet of 8.5x11 paper into thirds (like a letter) and then in half. Number each folded section on the blank sheet of paper with the numbers 1 to 6. This will give you a square for each of the Web sites you selected above.

3 Quickly sketch each of the pages you listed in Step 1. This should only take 30 seconds to a minute per thumbnail sketch. You don't have to be a great artist to do this.

Rough Sketches

Once graphic designers have sketched several ideas as thumbnails, they usually choose one or two of the thumbnails to develop further. This more developed sketch is called a **rough sketch**. A rough sketch still uses greeking and very abbreviated lines to represent things, but now they are a little more carefully drawn—proportions are more accurate, graphics are slightly more carefully drawn, and so on. Also, the rough sketch is a little larger—from 3x5 inches to a full page. Figure 6.1c shows a rough sketch.

4 Select one of the thumbnails you drew in Step 3. On a new blank sheet of paper take three to five minutes to create a more carefully drawn version *without looking at the original Web page*—your work should be based on the thumbnail you drew earlier. Include a few more details and be more cautious about proportions and the relative placement things on the page.

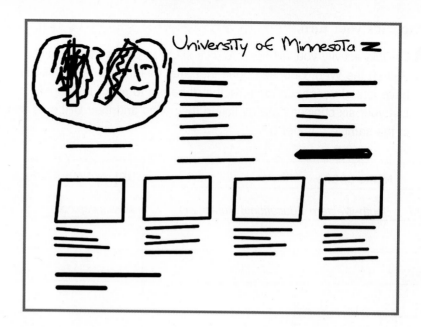

Figure 6.1c
A rough sketch made from a thumbnail sketch

How can the techniques you learned about in this activity—thumbnail and rough sketches—help you as you design your Web site for a high-tech online audience?

Design Desk *A Fourth Kind of Design*

There is another kind of design that is often not talked about, but can be as important. That is resource design or planning. By resource we mean what materials you need to get the job done. In the case of an automobile, that will include steel, copper, rubber, plastic, and lots of other materials, as well as the time and talents of many people. In the case of your Web site, we can usually just talk about the time involved to develop and create it.

Pretend for a moment that you've been hired by a company to design and produce their Web site. How much should you charge them for this service? How much time will it take? If you can answer these questions, you have a pretty good idea what resource planning is all about.

In fact, resource planning is actually just an edu-cated guess about what it's going to cost and how much time it will take. The more experience you have in design and development, the better your skill at guessing will become.

Here are some questions you will want to answer before you attempt to predict the time, money, and resource requirements of a Web project.

- *What kind of computer/Internet connection does the audience have?*
- *How big/small should my transmissions be?*
- *How simple/complicated should I make my pages?*
- *How much expertise do I need to have?*
- *How many hours will this take?*
- *What will it cost to finish it?*

Choosing a Visual Theme

You may think that with all the thinking about content, audience, and structure, that you don't have anything left to think about. Actually, everything you've been planning up to this point leads into this final step. You must now select a **visual theme** for your site.

A visual theme will help you make choices about the visual "look" of the Web site you are creating. A theme helps keep the "look and feel" of your site consistent from one page to the next, even though the content from page to page is different. Application of a theme is what brings about style.

Choosing a Theme

Choosing a theme can be the hardest and yet the most fun activity in this book because it can be drawn from virtually anything that your Web site's content reminds you of. Here are a few examples to help get your creative juices flowing:

- If you were doing a Web site on archaeology, you might make your Web site look like an Indiana Jones movie poster, with bright, sweeping orange titles and adventuresome graphics (like a picture of a whip or Indy's hat) because that fictional movie character was an archaeologist.

- In developing a Web site about a 1940s style of clothing, your theme might be the music of the 1940s because that was the last time those clothes were popular. Doing so would lead you to choose sights and sounds for your Web site from the music of that era—big bands and jazz.

- It might be that in doing a Web site about ants, you choose a military theme because ants remind you of soldiers. In this case, you could choose khaki colors and military graphics that remind you of the army. You might also put a lot of rigid structure into your site to remind people of the rigid order in the military.

As you can probably see, your theme can be connected with your content in a variety of ways. The important thing is that the theme should get your audience's attention and communicate your message well.

HOT TIP
Team Up!

It is best to brainstorm possible Web site themes with a team of people. Several people can create more ideas than a single person all by themselves. And, one idea can lead to another, and another, and another—until just the right one emerges. Get with a partner or small group and take turns doing the activity for each person in the group. If you are doing this activity as a team, work with your team to come up with ideas.

1. To help you choose a theme for your Web site, start by reviewing your design document. Read all the decisions you have already made (your audience, purpose, message, structure, and so on) and ask, "What does my Web site remind me of? What theme could best contain all of my ideas for this Web site?"

2. Take a few minutes with your partner or group to think of every idea you can that is associated with your site. You may either write your ideas down in your design document under a new heading called: *Web Site Theme Ideas. (Note: You may sketch your ideas as thumbnails if you prefer.)*

Design Desk

Poor Theme Ideas

When evaluating an idea for a visual theme, use what you think the audience's reaction will be to judge whether it is good or bad. Here are here are some not-so-great ideas for Web site themes:

A site about "new wave" music might use pictures of the ocean, that is, of "waves," as the theme. This kind of relationship is called a visual pun—new wave music has nothing to do with the ocean, but we're punning on the word wave. The problem is that the visual pun may be too subtle: The audience may not get it.

If someone were trying to make the point that math is fun, they might use a circus themes: bright colors (especially red) clowns, elephants, tents, popcorn. Even though the stated purpose of the site is to show that math is fun, a large majority of viewers may think the association of "math" with "circus" is incongruous or even nonsensical. They may not get the connection and may be confused by it, "Why is this circus Web site talking about math?"

This is a chance for you to brainstorm. While you are brainstorming, there are no bad ideas, so just write everything down. Do this for each member of the group, if they are working on different Web site designs. Often when brainstorming, one idea will lead to another (some people call this "idea hitchhiking"). Use this to generate lots of ideas. Don't stop until you have at least six to ten ideas listed in your design document.

3 Once you have lots of good ideas, you must weed out the bad ones from the good ones. Narrow down your ideas and prioritize your top six ideas. Delete the rest. You only need six themes for the next step.

4 You should now have a good list of six possible themes. Write a number to the left of each one which represents the ones you like best, 1 for your first choice, 2 for your second choice, and so on.

5 Take out a sheet of paper and fold it as you did in Activity 6.1, creating six boxes on the page.

6 Draw a thumbnail sketch of what you think your Web site's welcome page could look like if you applied the six themes you identified in Step 4. Sketch the first theme's possible welcome page in the first box, the second theme's welcome page in the second box, and so on, until you have a proposed welcome page for each theme. As you draw, imagine what your entire Web site might look like if based on each of these six themes.

7 Show the six thumbnail sketches to your team and gauge their reactions to your welcome page design ideas.

8 Based on your team's input and your own reaction to your ideas, pick one of the themes to use in the presentation design of your Web site.

9 Create a new entry in your design document called *Final Theme Decision*. Explain your theme and why you have decided to go with that particular theme. (You will create a rough drawing of your welcome page and you will apply your theme to your entire Web site in the next activity.)

10 Resave your design document.

THINKING ABOUT TECHNOLOGY: THEMES ON THE BIG SCREEN

Visual themes are taken from real life. Many of these true-to-life experiences are found in the movies. What themes have you seen in recent movies that project the high-tech themes of our information society?

Elements of a User Interface

Objective:
In this lesson, you will plan foreground and background colors, images, content, links, and other user interface features into your theme's design.

Now that you have selected a visual theme for your Web site, you must apply the design and create an overall look for your Web site presentation. You will want to plan the pieces or elements that are going to make up the various parts of your page.

Before you begin to apply your visual theme, you must consider three additional elements. Each Web page must have:

- A background that reflects the theme
- Foreground elements that reflect the theme
- Other elements that support the theme

Backgrounds: Colors or Images

On a Web page you have two choices for backgrounds: change the background's color, or add a background graphic. In the case of colors, you simply choose a color, and that is it. However, a background graphic in a Web page is often **tiled**, that is, repeated over and over again so that it forms a pattern. Since either the color or the pattern could overwhelm what is in the foreground, you have to be very careful that you choose colors or pictures that contrast well with whatever you put in front of them.

Foregrounds: Content and Links

The foreground is the page content. It will contain text and images to represent your message to your audience. Some of the text or graphics may be acting as headings, some as content, some as functional parts of the page, like hyperlinks to other pages. The list of foreground elements might include the elements displayed in Figure 6.3a, including:

- Titles
- Headings
- Subheadings
- Sidebars
- Body text (the paragraphs that make up the content of the site)

- Illustrations (graphics to support the content of the site)
- Captions (descriptions of the graphics)

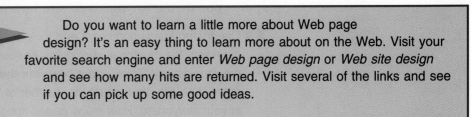

Do you want to learn a little more about Web page design? It's an easy thing to learn more about on the Web. Visit your favorite search engine and enter *Web page design* or *Web site design* and see how many hits are returned. Visit several of the links and see if you can pick up some good ideas.

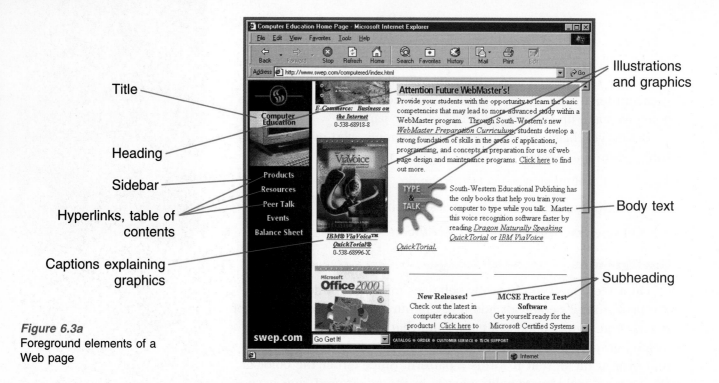

Title

Heading

Sidebar

Hyperlinks, table of contents

Captions explaining graphics

Illustrations and graphics

Body text

Subheading

Figure 6.3a
Foreground elements of a Web page

Other Elements

In addition to text and pictures, you can have other elements on a page: buttons, hyperlinks, search tools, navigation bars, table of contents, and other interactive and navigation elements (refer to Figure 6.3a). These are often created in HTML and JavaScript, useful tools that you may want to learn more about.

Applying Your Theme

Your job is to apply your selected theme to the elements on your page. When you made your thumbnails and rough sketches, you may have included some of the elements mentioned above. Reading may have brought other ideas to mind. In this activity, you will redraw your thumbnails for your Web site starting with your welcome page. You will need to construct your theme as you go along. This will give you a chance to brainstorm your visual design in light of the graphic theme you have chosen.

In this activity, take the time to turn your thumbnail sketches of your Web site pages into rough design drawings as instructed in Activity 6.1, Step 4. In your rough sketches, include any additional elements you may have missed. Plan the graphics, foreground and background elements, text, and navigation tools that will help you apply your theme to your Web site in a powerful way.

1 Open your design document and look at your storyboard pages. Compare them with the thumbnail sketch you created for your welcome page in the previous activity. Think about how your theme can apply across your entire Web site, then count the number of Web pages you have planned in your storyboard. How many pages appear on your storyboard?

Chapter 6 Presentation Design

2 Fold several sheets of paper into six squares and create as many thumbnail boxes as you have Web pages in your storyboard. If you have 24 Web pages planned, you will need to fold four sheets of paper.

3 Create a thumbnail sketch of each Web page you have identified in your storyboard. As you draw, imagine what your individual Web site may look like if you apply your theme to every page. Use your welcome page thumbnail as a guide.

4 In your design document, explain how you have applied your theme to your thumbnail sketches under the heading: *Application of the Design Theme to Web Site.* In your description, list and explain the background, foreground, and other elements you have sketched into your thumbnails of your Web site.

5 Save your additions to your design document.

THINKING ABOUT TECHNOLOGY: IN OVER YOUR HEAD?

As you plan the elements of your Web site, you will soon realize that without help, you may not be able to create the site you are thinking about. What types of highly trained experts will you need to create your ideal Web site? What high-tech tools will your experts use to create the ideal site?

SCOOP

Most Web page designers today used software tools to help them create their Web sites. One of the more popular Web page tools is Microsoft FrontPage, and there are many other outstanding Web site creation tools and HTML editors. At the bottom of some Web sites the Webmaster might tell you which software tool was used to create the site. Keep your eyes peeled for a useful tool to help you create your future Web sites.

ACTIVITY

6.4

Objective:

In this lesson, you will learn how a design grid can help you organize the unity, balance, and proportion of your Web pages.

A Grid for Everything

You have now identified a visual theme and a created thumbnail sketches of each of your Web pages. You now need to organize your Web site elements on each page in more detail. Your thumbnail sketches are first attempts, giving you a quick idea of what you want to do with the graphical aspects of your Web site.

In this activity you will create a rough sketch of each Web page on a full sheet of paper. If you have 24 pages planned in your storyboard, you will need 24 pieces of paper. Before you begin, consider these principles and how you can apply them to complete the visual look of your Web site.

Organizing Space by Using a Grid

The designers of paper documents like magazines and newspapers have learned a handy rule: that if you create grids into which you place your information, it will look more organized. A **grid** is just a bunch of vertical and horizontal gridlines (never diagonal) that you can use to organize your page. The lines aren't really there. They are just guidelines, like using a ruler to line things up, and then, after they are lined up, taking the ruler away. See Figure 6.4a for an example.

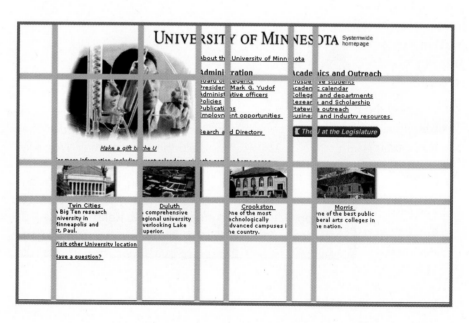

Figure 6.4a

A Web page with gridlines drawn in

Your Web site's visitors never see the lines in your grid; the lines are implied by how things are lined up and organized on your page.

A grid isn't the only way to organize material on a page, but it is one of the best and easiest. And if you use it right, it will help you with important design principles like unity, balance, and proportion.

Unity means that all the elements on your page look like they belong together. This is achieved by making them look similar (similar styles or colors) and placing them on the page so that they look "comfortable" around each other. The grid can give each item a "home" where it will be placed well.

Balance is like a see saw in a playground. The elements on the page must always balance. That doesn't mean that they must be equal weight on both sides (though sometimes it does). On a see saw, you can have a heavy adult held up by a small child if the child is at the far end of the see saw, and the adult is near the center on the other side.

Similarly, you can place "light" items (light text, light-colored or small graphics) far from the center, and have them balance a "heavy" item (large, dark graphics or heavy text) placed closer to the center. Having equally weighted items result in symmetrical balance; unequally weighted items result in asymmetrical balance—but they're both balanced! The center line (a vertical line down the middle of your screen on your grid) can help you balance the elements on your page.

Proportion means things look like they are the right size. You've probably seen drawings by small children where the head is as large as the rest of the body. These look funny because they are out of proportion (disproportionate). If you make something large that should be small, or something small that your Web site visitors can tell should be large, the result will be a feeling that something in your sight is not quite right (some artists do this on purpose for a humorous effect). Grids can help identify where something is disproportionate. Examples might be heading that are too big or too small, graphics that take up too much or too little space on the screen, and so on.

1 Examine the thumbnails you have created for your Web page. Start with your welcome page thumbnail. Think about how you can convert this thumbnail into a rough design sketch as you did in Activity 6.1.

2 Create a rough sketch of the welcome page on your Web site. On a sheet of blank paper, draw frames for your rough sketches by drawing simple rectangles to represent the screens. Use a ruler to make them straight, and draw them in black or some other dark color. Transfer your welcome page thumbnail sketch to your new rough design sketch. Draw lines on the rough sketch for each element, showing how each element lines up and is balanced with the other elements. As you draw them, always continue the lines to both edges of the screen (top and bottom or right and left). Use a ruler or straight edge for these lines. Only horizontal and vertical lines are allowed. (If you have one, use a light blue or other light-colored pencil for these lines.)

Complete the rough sketch by drawing in the rest of the details of the page. Use colored pencils if you like, or create the rough sketch on a computer with a drawing program.

As you draw, try to identify examples of unity, balance, and proportion. On the back of the page, write a short description of where you noticed any one of these three important design principles.

3 Once you have your welcome page designed the way you want it, create rough sketches for each Web page you are planning for your Web site using the same thinking that you applied in Step 2 above. Complete your rough sketches by filling in the details: sketches of graphics or photos, greeking for the text, headings, and so on. As in Step 2 above, draw with a ruler or straight edge two rectangles to represent the frames for your Web pages. Remember you are trying to achieve unity, balance, and proportion.

Having completed your final rough sketches of your Web site, you are ready to build your Web pages. You can use FrontPage or another HTML editor or Web authoring tool to help you, or you can create the pages by hard-coding HTML yourself. Whatever tools you decide to use to apply your design, you will have a clear direction, and you will know what you want to see. You can now visualize how your site will look. You may need help creating certain elements of your Web pages, but that's okay. It takes teamwork to create great Web sites.

In the chapters that follow, you will explore how to write the text and how to import graphics into your Web site. Applying your design may be the most fun you have had. It will be exciting to see your Web site theme come together.

THINKING ABOUT TECHNOLOGY: HIGH-TECH GRIDS

Macintosh and Windows desktops can become really messy. Can you use a grid to organize your computer's desktop? Will this make things easier to find?

Net Ethics   RESPECT the Web: The Ethics Test

Unethical people can abuse the Web. Many people without a sense of community values place objectionable material such as pornography, hate group information, racially biased material, or prejudiced information on the Web. Some lie about products or services. Other try to cheat people by using the Web to promote nonexistent causes or scans.

What are the things you value? Write your values down in a list and let this list guide you as you create your Web pages. By the same token, when you create your Web pages you need to ask yourself the following ethical questions. If the answer to any of these questions is no, then you need to change your Web page accordingly:

• Does my page conform to my values?
• Is the information on my page accurate and correct?
• Is my message honest?
• Is the information I am sharing beneficial?
• Is the information I'm sharing legal for me to share with others?

WEB VOCABULARY

Define the following terms:

1. *thumbnail sketches*   4. *visual theme*   7. *unity*

2. *greeking*   5. *tiled*   8. *balance*

3. *rough sketch*   6. *grid*   9. *proportion*

WEB REVIEW

Give a short answer to the following questions:

1. *Why are thumbnail and rough design sketches important to a Web page designer?*

_____

_____

_____

2. *Why do Web designers use themes to help guide the presentation design of their Web sites?*

_____

_____

_____

3. *How are balance and the portion related to each other?*

_____

_____

_____

4. *How do gridlines assist a Web page designer?*

_____

_____

5. *In terms of Web design, what does the term "unity" mean?*

_____

_____

WEB SITE PRESENTATION

Wally Woodword is about to launch his corporation's Web site at **www.wallywoodworks.com**. However, not being an artist himself, he is concerned about how the Web site will look. He doesn't want to spend a lot of money and end up with an ugly Web site. He has asked you for help. He would like to see some possible thumbnail sketches of how his Web site may appear. Prepare six thumbnail sketches and a rough design sketch of the welcome page for Wally to approve.

WEB SITE Under Construction Work Teams Ahead

Wally Woodword would like to know what his competition is doing online. In a team of three or four people, use your search skills and find at least five Web pages dedicated cabinet making, woodworking, or to making furniture for homes. Have each member of the team select one of the sites you have found and grid it. Create a rough design of these pages applying the grid system that you learned how to create in Activity 6.4. Show how space is organized on that Web page. As a team, prepare the presentation for Wally Woodword, demonstrating to him how his site can be made the most attractive and exciting of all the woodworking sites on the Web.

WRITING ABOUT TECHNOLOGY Planning for Design

With what you know about Web design at this point, write a 100-word answer to one of the following options:

Option 1.   How has your design document helped you keep track of your Web site development plans?

Option 2.   Now that you have planned the entire scope of your Web site, what resources and talents of would you need to create this Web site to your satisfaction? Make a list of the kind of talented people you will need in order to complete an outstanding Web site following your recommendations in your design document.

Option 3.   Which of these three elements of design do you feel are the most important in the Web site development process: information design, interaction design, or presentation design? Explain your answer.

Some of the important things you may need to learn next include HTML and JavaScript. The *HTML & JavaScript Programming Concepts* text by South-Western Educational Publishing may be just what you need to get started with these exciting tools.

Preparing Your Web Site

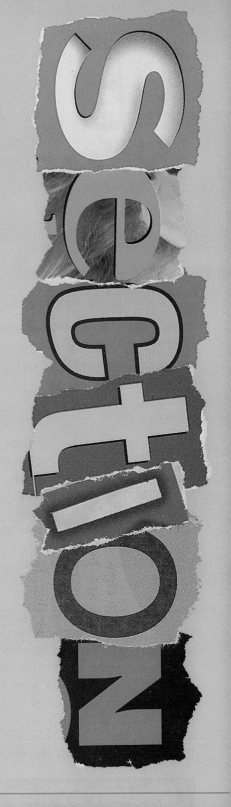

You're nearly done. You've thought and written and drawn the design for your Web site. You've completed information design, interaction design, and a good deal of presentation design. You only have a couple of things left to do.

Your Web page will be made up of words and pictures. How are you supposed to prepare your text? How do you get the pictures ready for you Web site? This section will show you how to do that.

Though not strictly part of design, these important skills are necessary to the completion of a high-quality Web site. When these two items are taken care of for every page in your site, you will have nothing left to do but put it all together!

Creating Text

Chapter Objectives:

In this chapter, you will focus on creating your Web site's content. After reading Chapter 7, you will be able to:

1. write your Web site's text in rough draft form.

2. edit your Web site's text.

Web Terms

traffic

spiders

database

consistency errors

Spend any amount of time on the Web and you are bound to run into hundreds of Web sites overflowing with fancy images, but lacking any real substance. These Web sites are called eye candy—they are fun to look at, but they do not provide anything meaningful to read.

To create a content-rich Web site, you have to know your audience, you have to identify the message you want your Web site to convey, and you have to ensure that your message matches the needs of your audience. Because of this, you have to focus on *both* the style *and* the substance of each of the Web pages you design.

Which is more important, the style (your Web site's look and feel) or the substance (your content)? The answer is almost always *substance*. After all, how can you expect to meet the needs of your audience if your Web site has nothing to say? In fact, unless you are designing a Web site whose message can be conveyed almost totally with pictures (for example, a Web site for an art gallery or an electronic version of a school's yearbook), your main focus will be on the words that comprise the substance of your Web site.

Design Ethics   *Using the Words of Others*

Thanks to the World Wide Web, you now have the ability to access tens of millions of documents around the world. You may be tempted to "borrow" text or ideas from some of these documents as you develop your Web site. If you do borrow text or an idea from another document, you must document it just as if you had copied it from a book. In other words, you *must* give credit where credit is due. Plagiarism is plagiarism, whether the material is printed or presented online. Why do you think it is unethical to borrow text or an idea from another document without giving credit? What harm could result from your doing this?

First Draft: Write the Text for Your Pages

ACTIVITY

7.1

Objective:
In this lesson, you will learn how to create the first draft of your Web site's text.

The underlying goal of every Web page designer is to create Web pages that generate *traffic*. Traffic refers to the number of people who visit a Web page or Web site during a particular period. Successful Web sites experience enormously high traffic (at the time of this writing, Yahoo!'s traffic exceeds 25 million visitors a month). Unsuccessful Web sites experience little or no traffic.

What separates high-traffic sites from low-traffic ones? A key factor is how well a particular Web site meets the needs of its audience. After all, would you want to visit a football Web site that did not mention a single thing about football or a basic arithmetic Web site that expected you to know calculus? If you tailor the content of your Web pages to meet the needs of your audience, you will be rewarded with increasing traffic. Granted, your traffic may not be as high as Yahoo!'s, but the better you serve your audience, the more popular your Web pages will become.

This is why a rule of good Web page design is to know your audience. If you know your audience, and you tailor the content of your Web pages to meet their needs, your Web pages will be both successful and popular.

The Format of Web Page Text

Web pages and term papers are similar in their format. Both have an introduction, a body, and (sometimes) a conclusion. The introduction is where you introduce your audience to the topic you are going to discuss. The body is where you discuss your topic, point by point. Finally, the conclusion is where you summarize what you have already said. As you go over the parts of your Web site, take time to develop your content according to the guidelines.

The First Sentence

The most important part of any Web page—and certainly the most difficult part to write—is the introduction. Obviously, the first paragraph, and especially the very first sentence, of your Web page will be one of the first things your audience sees. It could also be the first, and possibly only, introduction to your Web page that search engine users will see. To understand why this is, you have to understand a little bit about how Internet search engines work.

There are literally tens of millions of Web pages on the World Wide Web, and that number is growing daily. In fact, there are so many Web pages available it is almost impossible for anyone to locate a new Web page without the help of a search engine. A search engine is a type of software, usually accessed through a particular Web site (like *www.webcrawler.com*), that lets you search the Web for pages whose content contains certain key words or phrases.

Most search engines use automated programs called **spiders** that "crawl" around the Web looking for new Web pages. When a spider finds a new Web page, it sends information about that Web page back to the search engine. The search engine then adds this information to its collection of information about millions of other Web pages. This collection of information, called a **database**, is organized for rapid searching and retrieval. So, when you use a search engine, you aren't really searching the Web itself, you are searching through that search engine's database of Web sites.

What sort of information do spiders report to search engines? Well, obviously it varies, but almost all spiders report the Web page's title and the first few sentences.

When you conduct a keyword search using your favorite search engine, the search engine scans its database looking for any Web pages that match your search terms and then displays the information it has on those Web pages that match what you are looking for. To keep from flooding you with information, the search engines usually only show you a list of Web sites, with each page's title and a brief description of the page's content. In many cases, that description comes directly from the page's first sentence.

As you can see, your page's first sentence could be the first, and possibly only, introduction to your Web page that search engine users will see. This is why choosing a good first sentence is very important.

Figure 7.1a shows you the results of a keyword search for the words *British Monarchy* using the AltaVista search engine. Figure 7.1.b shows you the first page that AltaVista found that matches those key words.

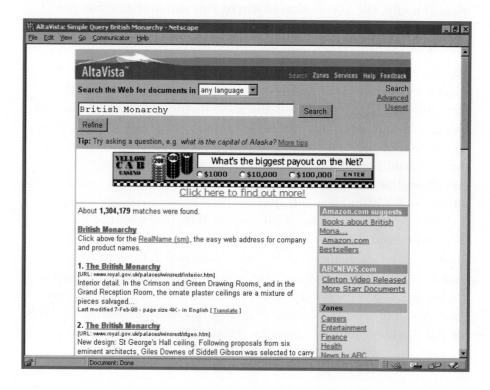

Figure 7.1a
The results of an AltaVista Search search for the key words "*British Monarchy*"

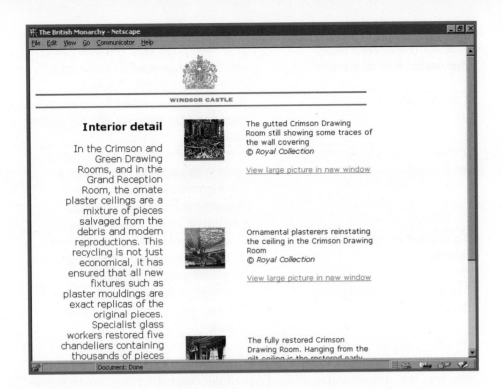

Figure 7.1b
The first page that AltaVista returned using a key word search for *"British Monarchy"* (*www.royal.gov.uk/palaces/ winsrest/interior.htm*)

Notice that the description of the first Web page AltaVista found is "Interior detail. In the Crimson and Green Drawing Rooms, and in the Grand Reception Room, the ornate plaster ceilings are a mixture of pieces salvaged…" Now take a look at the first sentence in Figure 7.1b. It is identical.

As we said earlier, most search engines display only the first one or two sentences of the Web pages they archive. If you want to generate traffic to your pages from these search engines, the first sentence of your Web page has to clearly explain your page's topic. In other words, the first sentence should grab your audience's attention, tell them what your topic is, and interest them in what you have to say.

Good and Bad First Sentences

How can you write a good first sentence? Well, practice makes perfect. You can also learn from bad examples. Table 7.1a gives you examples of both good and bad first sentences. Look at each carefully and try to figure out what makes the "bad" sentences bad and the "good" sentences good.

Design Desk *Word Processors or Web Page Editor Programs?*

Should you type your Web page's text in a word processor like Microsoft Word or Corel WordPerfect, or in a Web page editor program like Microsoft Front-Page or Adobe PageMill? The answer is: use a word processor—they have more powerful spell checkers. You can import the text or copy and paste it into the HTML editor later.

Bad First Sentences	Good First Sentences
This is my first Web page. I've never done one before.	This Web page tells you everything you could ever want to know about the 1979 Pittsburgh Steelers.
I like mittens.	Welcome to the mitten home page, your one-stop shop for all your mitten needs.
This is the introduction to my Web page.	This page shows you the elements of good Web page text authoring: a good introductory sentence, well thought-out body text, and a short summation of the topics presented.
To find out more about us, read this.	This is the information headquarters for Union High School's Renegade Regiment marching band.
I hope to get a good grade in school.	This Web page explains the time-honored secrets to earning good grades.

Table 7.1a
Examples of bad and good introductory sentences

Hardly anyone has written a good introductory sentence on the first try. It's almost impossible. Lots of successful writers write *something* to fill the place where the good introductory sentence will go, write the rest of the page, and then go back and write the *real* introductory sentence.

Write an introductory sentence and then review it. If there were nothing else but the introductory sentence on your page, would your intended audience know they were in the right place? If so, you're getting closer to a good introductory sentence. If not, take some time to rewrite it.

For example, take another look at the first sentence that appears in Figure 7.1b. Does the phrase "interior detail" grab your attention, tell you what the topic is, or interest you in what this particular Web page has to say? Clearly, Figure 7.1b shows you a good example of a weak first sentence.

Now that you get the idea, try a search of your own.

1. Open your Web browser.

2. Key in the following address in the appropriate box: *www.altavista.com*

3. Key in the search term *Norse Mythology* and click on the Search button.

4. Review the descriptions of the Web pages that AltaVista finds. How many descriptions make sense? How many descriptions interest you? What could the authors of these Web pages do to make these descriptions clearer and more appealing?

5. Conduct another search, this time looking for a keyword or phrase that interests you. How many of these new descriptions make sense?

6. Write a few first sentences for your own Web page and work with them until you get one you like.

The Body Text

Once you have chosen a good introductory sentence, your next step is to write the main text of your Web page. Like the body text of a term paper or report, this is where you present the facts, comments, and information you want to share with your audience.

In Chapter 5 you identified your audience, created an outline that showed your general message or focus, and chose your Web site's organizational scheme.

To write the body text of your Web page, you simply need to transform your outline into an actual document. In effect, your Web page's body text is nothing more than a detailed report that you are writing for your audience.

Whether you write your Web page's main text on paper or on a computer using a word processor, you need to keep your audience in mind and make sure that everything you write focuses on meeting their needs. In fact, you need to remember that most of your audience may not know as much about your topic as you do. This leads us to another rule of good Web page design: if there is a chance that someone in your audience will not understand a certain part of your Web page, either explain that part in full or don't write it. This rule is sometimes called the "lowest common denominator" rule—in other words, you should write your body text so that it is understandable to even the most novice of readers.

For example, let's pretend that you are writing a Web page that focuses on NASA. A good Web page designer would explain that NASA stands for the National Aeronautics and Space Administration (and a *really* good Web page designer would explain a little of NASA's history).

One last thing to remember as you write your body text is that the Web is international. Writing something like "hop on the Interstate and drive to your nearest 7-11" will probably make no sense to someone outside the United States (after all, there are no Interstates or 7-11s in Germany). If your audience is international, make sure that your Web page's body text includes language that is universal.

7 Write a draft of the main body of your Web page.

The Conclusion

The last part of a paper is the conclusion, where you restate the points you made earlier. With Web pages, the conclusion part is optional (many Web page designers omit it altogether). The decision on whether or not to include a conclusion should be based on what you think your audience will expect.

8 Write a brief conclusion to your Web page text.

Think about some of the papers or reports you have recently written. Would any of them make good Web pages? What changes would you have to make to these papers or reports to ensure that appeal to the general public who surf the Web? What changes would you have to make to be sure that your papers or reports are understandable to international readers? What are the problems that could arise from putting your old papers and reports on the Web?

Design News — *Encyclopaedia Britannica Internet Guide*

The Encyclopaedia Britannica Web site recently created an Internet directory called "eBLAST" (*www.eblast.com*). To create their directory, Britannica reviewed over 2 million Web sites, looking for sites with "depth, accuracy, completeness, and utility of information." Britannica found only 125,000 sites whose content was of high enough quality to meet their standards.

Editing Your Text

ACTIVITY

7.2

Objective:
In this lesson, you will edit
your Web page's text.

Now that you have written the first draft of your Web site's text, it is time for you to "clean it up." This is actually a simple process, but it is one that many inexperienced Web page designers overlook.

Step One: Spell Check

One of the quickest ways to lose your audience (and annoy them) is to write a Web page that uses poor grammar or misspelled words. After all, would you trust a Web page that told you that "the bestest way to make mony fast iz too purchase our mony-making pro-ducks"?

So, the first and most crucial step in the editing process is to run your Web page's text through a spell checker. Fortunately, most word processors (like Corel WordPerfect and Microsoft Word) and even some HTML editor programs (like Adobe PageMill and Microsoft FrontPage) offer built-in spell checkers.

Spell checkers will not catch *every* misspelled or misused word, though, so it is a good idea to carefully examine each sentence in your Web page for misspelled and misused words. Here are some commonly misspelled or misused words:

- *You* and *Your.* This is a frequent typo on Web pages, and spell checkers will not catch it. A good example of this error appears in the sentence, "you need to make sure that you message matches your audience."

- *Two, To,* and *Too. Two* is a number; *to* is a preposition; and *too* means "also."

- *There, They're,* and *Their. There* is a direction; *they're* is a contraction of "they are"; and, *their* means "belonging to them."

- *Its* and *It's. Its* means "belonging to it"; *it's* is a contraction for "it is."

- *You're* and *Your. You're* is short for "you are" or "you were"; *your* means "belonging to you."

- *All ready* and *Already. All ready* means to be prepared; *already* means "previously."

Spell checkers will also miss **consistency errors**. A consistency error occurs when you change your writing style from paragraph to paragraph or from page to page. The two biggest consistency errors involve pronoun use and contraction use:

- *Pronoun Use.* Starting a page in a plural voice ("we are glad you chose to visit our Web page") and then switching to singular ("if you have any questions, contact me at …"). Pick singular (I, me, mine, and so on) or plural (we, us, our, and so on), and then stick with it throughout your Web pages.

- *Contraction Use*. Switching between using contractions (I've, won't, you're) and not using contractions (I have, will not, you are). If you use contractions, use them throughout your Web site; if you don't use contractions, avoid them consistently.

1 Do a careful read to check for consistency errors in your Web text.

2 Run a careful spell check on your Web text.

Step Two: Expand Your Narrative

Now that you have checked the spelling of your text, the next step in the editing process is to expand on what you have already written. Reread each sentence in your Web page's text carefully and ask yourself if you have given enough information to make the material understandable to the most novice of readers. If you haven't, you'll need to expand on what you have written. Fill in the holes, but don't offer mountains of information.

This is also a good time to have your colleagues or another team in your class proofread a rough draft of your Web page's text. These people will be able to spot any typos you have missed, and they will also be able to tell you which parts of your Web page's text need to be revised or rewritten to make those parts more understandable.

3 Expand your Web page text as discussed above.

4 Have a colleague read through your text and make suggestions.

Step Three: Weed It Out

The third step in the editing process is to remove as many words as you can from your Web page. This may seem counterintuitive, especially after you just expanded your narrative in Step Two above. The reason you need to edit your text, though, is to save your audience's time. After all, why say, "After careful consideration of the entire situation, I have decided to decline your offer" when you can just as easily say, "Sorry, no?"

E. B. White said it in just four words: "Make every word tell." White was a highly educated professional writer. But notice how short his sentence is and how concise the words are. This leads us to the next thing you should do to edit your text: Take out every big word and replace it with a shorter, simpler word. Better yet, just take it out. Usually it won't be missed.

No, let's take our own advice on that last sentence: It won't be missed.

Here is a good example of how you can save your audience's time through editing:

Original Paragraph (150 words):

Writing a Web page is pretty easy. The only trick is that you have to know a few simple rules. One of the most important rules is that you have to know your audience. Once you have identified your audience, you need to make sure that the message of your

Web page matches your audience. After you have done that, you need to realize that if it would be easier on the audience if you divided your information into two or more pages, then divide your information into two or more pages. Of course, the opposite of this is true as well: if you don't need to divide your information into different Web pages, then you don't have to. Finally, if there is a chance that someone in your audience will not understand a certain part of your Web page, either explain that part in full or don't write it.

New Paragraph (62 words):

Writing a Web page is easy, provided you know a few rules. You must know your audience, and you must match your message to your audience. If you can easily divide your Web page's information into two or more pages, do it; if you can't, don't. Finally, ensure that the information on your Web page is understandable to everyone who views it.

Both paragraphs say the same thing, but the second one is shorter and much easier to read.

⑤ Look at your Web page text and carefully rework phrases and words until you have edited it down to a readable, essential core.

Step Four: Spell Check and Proofread (Again)

Now that you have radically changed your Web page's text, it is a good idea to spell check it and proofread it one last time. In fact, it is at this step that many professional Web designers spell check their text, proofread it, and then ask someone else to proofread their text just to be safe.

⑥ Do a final, careful proofread and spell check of your Web page text. Get help from your colleagues, if you want.

As you edit your Web page text, you will probably have a few questions about spelling and grammar. Fortunately, the Web can help you answer these questions:

⑦ Open your Web browser.

⑧ Key in the following address in the appropriate box: *www.yahoo.com.*

⑨ Key in the search term *English Grammar Usage* and click on the Search button.

⑩ When the search is complete, click on the *English: Grammar, Usage, and Style* category.

⑪ Click on a link that focuses on your question.

If your question is about spelling or definition of a word, visit the following address instead: *www.m-w.com/dictionary.htm.* This is the Merriam-Webster online dictionary.

HOT TIP
Web Addresses

Note that current links to most Web sites presented in this book can be found on the Web Page Design home page. Go to webdesign.swep.com. Remember that a Web address may change at any time. An address given in this book as an example may no longer be valid. If this is so, either access this book's home page for the current link or do a search to find a similar site.

THINKING ABOUT TECHNOLOGY: TEXT EDITING

How is the Web page text editing process different from what you have done when you edited papers or reports? How is it different? Do you think that cutting the amount of text significantly in your papers or reports help or hurt those documents? Why?

JUST THE FACTS

Just The Facts: The Power of Web Text

Every Web browser in the world is able to display Web page text. Not every Web browser, however, can display Web graphics. In fact, as a service to people with really slow Internet connections, both Netscape Navigator and Microsoft Internet Explorer have a built-in option that lets you view Web pages without having to view (and download) the graphics. If you want, you can later load the images individually.

Remember, your Web site's text can be viewed by everybody, regardless of their browser. Your Web site's graphics, however, can only be viewed by people who use graphical Web browsers and who have their graphical Web browsers set to automatically load and display images.

SCOOP

The Most Popular Web Sites? Search Engines!

According to *Relevant Knowledge*, in August 1998 five of the ten most popular Web sites in the world were search engines or directories: Yahoo! (number 1), Excite (number #6), Lycos (number #7), Infoseek (number #8), and AltaVista (number #10). To see this month's resultsthe most recent results, point your Web browser to *www.relevantknowledge.com/*

Putting It All Together

Creating Web sites with content that is both meaningful to your audience and that has something of substance to say isn't easy. To create a content-rich Web site, you have to know your audience, you have to identify the message you want your Web site to convey, and you have to ensure that your message matches the needs of your audience.

To understand how audience, message, and organization all come together to affect content, let's take a look at an example. The Bertrand Russell Intermediate High School Concert Choir has decided to create their own Web site. They have identified their primary audience:

- current choir members and their families

- past choir members

- people interested in joining the choir

- people interested in attending future choir performances

If we think about the needs of these four audiences, we see that each group has its own needs:

- Current choir members and their families want schedules and contact information.

- Past choir members want archive information about who was in their choir and what music they performed.

- People interested in joining the choir want information on how to join the choir, when it rehearses, and any auditioning information.

- People interested in attending future performances want schedule information, directions on how to get to the performances, and information about what music is going to be performed.

One structure that will really work for this Web site is a hierarchical structure. Figure 7.3a shows you the hierarchical structure for the Bertrand Russell Intermediate High School Choir's Web site. Notice that there are four Web pages—one for each of the audiences—along with a fifth, top-level Web page. This top-level page, called the welcome page, or the homepage, is the choir's main Web page. From the choir's home page, anyone is able to access the choir's four other Web pages.

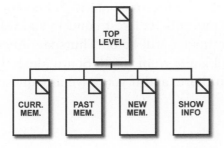

Figure 7.3a
Hierarchical structure of the Bertrand Russell Intermediate High School Choir's Web site

Design Desk

Some Rules of Good Web Page Design

- *Know your audience.*
- *Your message needs to match your audience.*
- *Divide your information into two or more pages if it's easier for your audience.*
- *If you don't need to divide your information into different Web pages, don't.*
- *If there is a chance that someone in your audience will not understand a certain part of your Web page, either explain that part in full or don't write it.*

Now that we have identified the basics of the audience, message, and organization for the choir's Web site text, it is time to write the text for each of the site's Web pages.

Writing the Text

Since we already have a rough outline for each of the Web site's pages (simply by identifying the needs of each of the Web site's audiences), the next step is to fill in the outline with specifics.

The following is the first draft of the Web page that focuses on meeting the needs of the people interested in attending future choir performances. Use what you have learned in Activities 7.1 and 7.2 to find the mistakes in this text. Check for a strong opening sentence, spelling, grammar, consistency, and complete information.

> **Concert Choir**. The Concert Choir will be performing again soon. Our next performance will be on August 7th. The performance will start at 7:00 PM. The performance will be held in the high school auditorium. The performance will be a caucophony of melodic and symphonic gloriosity. We'd love to see you there. If you have any questions, call me at 555-7981.

Okay, let's go through the checklist.

- Obviously, that first sentence has to go. The opener "Concert Choir" does not grab your attention, does not tell you what the page's topic is, nor does it particularly inspire interest in what this particular Web page has to offer. A much better first sentence would be something like: "The Bertrand Russell Intermediate High School Concert Choir proudly presents its latest concert extravaganza."

- The next four sentences have a few problems as well. While these sentences contain a lot of words, they don't offer much solid information. What day of the week is August 7th? How do you get to the high school auditorium? Is the concert free?

- The fifth sentence—"the performance will be a caucophony of melodic and symphonic gloriosity"—is downright silly. It contains a misspelled, misused word and a made-up word to boot.

- The last two sentences suffer from consistency errors. One sentence uses the word "we," and the next uses the word "me."

Cleaned up, the text for this Web page would read much better as:

> The Bertrand Russell Intermediate High School Concert Choir proudly presents its latest concert extravaganza. Our next free performance will be on Thursday, August 7th, in the high school auditorium (6636 South Mingo Road). We'd love to see you there, and if you have any questions call us at 555-1212.

That's it. You've just followed the Web page design process from audience identification to finished text!

Now that you're really good at this, try your hand at the following exercise.

1 Open your Web browser.

2 Key in the following address in the appropriate box: *netsquirrel.com/rha*

3 This page provides links to college and university residence hall associations (also known as "dorm councils" or "dorm governments") around the world. Pick three schools at random and visit their Web pages.

4 How good are each school's first sentences? On a sheet of paper, describe the spelling errors, detail how these Web pages could have explained things better, and explain how parts of these Web pages could be shortened.

5 Go back to each of the three pages you have chosen and ask yourself, "If I were visually impaired and could only hear the words on this particular page without seeing the pictures, would this page still make sense?" How could the designers of these pages have made their pages more accessible to the visually impaired?

THINKING ABOUT TECHNOLOGY: AUDIENCE IDENTIFICATION

What would happen if you did not identify the audience for the Web sites you create? Would not identifying your audience make choosing a message easier or harder? Give an example of a Web site whose message is so universal that its creators need not worry about identifying its audience. Is this example the exception or the rule?

Net Ethics   RESPECT the Web: The Correct Test

This test may seem obvious, but it is very important nonetheless. Use the following list as a test for each Web page you create:

- Are all the words spelled correctly?
- Does the writing conform to the rules of grammar?
- Do all the hyperlinks work?
- Is all the data presented on the Web site correct and accurate?

CHAPTER REVIEW

WEB VOCABULARY

Define the following terms:

1. traffic

2. spiders

3. database

4. consistency errors

WEB REVIEW

Give a short answer to the following questions:

1. How could not meeting the expectations of your audience lead to lower traffic for your pages?

2. Why is your Web page's introductory sentence so important (give at least two reasons)?

3. Think about E. B. White's phrase, "Make every word tell." Can you improve it? How might a politician write that sentence?

4. Why are short words better than long ones?

5. How could identifying your Web site's audience actually help determine what your Web site's message is going to be? Give an example other than the Bertrand Russell Intermediate High School Concert Choir Web site example.

Net PRoJeCt

It is now time to finalize your Web site's text. Apply what you know about text and compose the required text to add to your Web pages.

WEB SITE  ////// | Under Construction Work Teams Ahead | //////

Don't work alone! There is a lot that you may not know. Others on your team may be able to help you with what belongs on the various pages of your site.

Take your completed Web site text to your team and have them evaluate it. Work as a tam to foster constructive criticism and help each other make meaningful changes to the test, including rewriting, reorganizing, or placing text in different places in the site. Your team may also help you see where your text does not cover the subject adequately, or where it covers material outside the defined scope of the Web site.

Perhaps the team can work together to edit and improve on Web site project at a time. Then the entire team can move to the next project, and the next, until every member of the team has an outstanding individual Web site text.

WRITING ABOUT TECHNOLOGY: Is Content Really King?

With what you know about Web design at this point, write a 100-word response to one of the following:

Option 1.   If a picture is traditionally worth a thousand words, give five reasons why you think the content of a Web site is more important than its graphics.

Option 2.   Explain the steps you need to take when you create the text for your Web site.

_____

_____

_____

_____

_____

_____

_____

_____

_____

_____

The Whys and Wherefores of Web Graphics

Chapter Objectives:

In this chapter, you will learn different roles graphics play in a Web page. After reading Chapter 8 you will be able to:

1. determine how graphics can become part of a Web site's message.

2. examine how graphics are used as interface elements.

3. discover how the theme can be enhanced by graphics.

4. understand the concepts of additive and subtractive colors, pixels, palettes, and dithering.

5. create GIF and JPEG graphics.

Web Terms

inline graphic

icons

additive color

subtractive color

RGB

pixel

resolution

aliasing

anti-aliasing

color depth

palette

dithering

GIF

JPEG

Graphics Made the Web Popular

Can you imagine the Web without graphics? Most people can't, but the early Web was a text-only environment. The original Web browsers allowed only text to be displayed and hyperlinked. But starting with a software program called Mosaic in 1994, browsers began to allow **inline graphics**; that is, graphics in the same line as the HTML text. The Mosaic project was housed at the University of Illinois at Urbana-Champaign. One computer science student who worked on Mosaic was Marc Andreessen.

Andreessen went on to help create one of the most influential Internet-based companies, Netscape, which is now part of America Online. Netscape Communications Corporation replaced Mosaic with a more powerful and efficient graphical browser, called Netscape Navigator. Later, Microsoft made its Internet Explorer (IE) browser available to customers. Both of these browsers display graphics brilliantly and present other multimedia elements in an exciting way.

To make your Web pages communicate well, you will want to add graphics to them. Your graphics must look good or they will get in the way of your message.

The Roles Graphics Play

Graphics can have several different roles in a Web page, but the most common are

- part of the message
- one of the user interface elements
- part of the theme

You should always have a good reason for using a graphic image. Each graphic must have a purpose. If not, your users will wonder what purpose the graphic serves, or even worse, they might be confused by the Web site graphics.

Graphics as Part of the Message

Graphics that are part of the message tend to be:

- large
- photographic
- important

Large graphics are used when they *are* the message itself. In other words, when the message the Web site wishes to communicate is best said with a picture, it is okay to use a large graphic. Because they are key to the message, some graphics can legitimately take up a lot of space on the page. After all, the page is about the image, about visual messaging. In fact, some Web pages have nothing but pictures with just a small amount of descriptive text.

Imagine that you just dropped in from another planet and someone here was trying to help you understand what a cat is. Which would you think would be more informative: a photograph of a cat or a cartoon cat? Some pictures are best represented by a photographic image.

Photographic images are very detailed. Web graphics are often photograph-like: providing lots of detail like a photograph. The camera does not leave things out selectively; the added detail lends reality and additional value to the graphic.

We've all heard the saying, "A picture is worth a thousand words." We'd like to modify that somewhat—the *right* picture is worth *at least* a thousand words. (The wrong picture may take a thousand words to explain, but it isn't worth very much.) That is why a good picture (one that is relevant to your subject) is definitely worth a lot.

It is a sad fact that many people will not plow through too much text on a computer screen unless they're *really* interested in it. Because our minds react to visual stimuli, you can move a lot of information and emotion into the mind with a picture. The images you choose can supply the most important part of your message.

If you created a Web site about the performance of a play, you might use pictures of the cast members in their costumes to show who was in the play. In this instance, the pictures are representations of the people in the play, since you can't have the live actors themselves hanging around for the advertising.

Generally, when a graphic is standing in for something, it is a representation. Sometimes, a picture represents a group of things or a type of thing. For example, if a Web site contained pictures of animals, you can probably guess what clicking on individual graphics of a dog, cat, and fish would lead to.

The neat thing about representations is that they are usually pretty easy to understand. They can often stand alone without any other explanation. Representations are most often used as part of the message of the Web page.

In this first activity, you will identify three pages on the Web that meet these three criteria discussed above:

1 Search the Web with your favorite Internet search engine or by browsing an index site like Yahoo! Find a Web page you like that uses a *large* image to dominate its message. List the title of the Web page and its URL here, and explain how the image is used. Think about how you might use an image of this sort in your Web site.

Large image Web page title:_____

Large image Web page URL:_____

How is the image used?_____

2 Find a Web page you like that uses a *photographic* image. List the title of the Web page and its URL here, and explain how the image is used. Think about how you might use an image of this sort in your Web site.

Photographic image Web page title:_____

Photographic image Web page URL:_____

How is the image used?_____

3 Find a Web page you like that uses graphics to visually demonstrate that some specific element has great importance. List the title of the Web page and its URL here, and explain how the image is used. Think about how you might use an image of this sort in your Web site.

Important image Web page title:_____

Important image Web page URL:_____

How is the image used?_____

Graphics as User Interface and Navigation Elements

It is always more fun to have nice graphics serve as your user interface and navigation elements.

User interface elements let you know where you are in the Web site and where you can go. (Review Activities 5.3 and 5.4 from Chapter 5.) User interface elements are often **icons**, small symbolic graphics that help the Web page visitor understand what each will do when selected. For instance, on your browser toolbar itself, you'll probably have no problem finding the Print icon. To make obscure icons a little more clear, icons are often accompanied by text, such as the word *print* under the appropriate icon on many Web browsers. To find graphic images that are user interface elements, you should ask yourself, "Which graphics help me know where I am or where I can go?"

Another kind of graphic is often overlooked by beginners. These are called *text graphics*. These are often used as banners. Because the fonts and kinds of text that can be displayed on a Web page are limited, text is often actually drawn by artists and converted to a graphic image. This technique allows the designers to create very attractive text and logos with some special effects. Of course, the downside to using text graphics is that they download much more slowly that straight text. But that is a price most Web designers are willing to pay to achieve exactly the look they want on a Web page.

4 Search the Web for a page you like that uses graphics to expertly facilitate navigation and user interactions. List the title of the Web page and its URL here, and explain how the graphics are used. Think about how you might use these sorts of images in your Web site.

Navigation Web page title: _____

Navigation Web page URL: _____

How are these images used? _____

_____

5 Find a Web page you like that uses a graphic to display text, as in its banner. List the title of the Web page and its URL here, and explain how the graphic text is used. Think about how you might use graphic text in your Web site:

Graphic text Web page title: _____

Graphic text Web page URL: _____

How is the graphic text used? _____

Graphics as Part of the Theme

Graphics that enhance a Web site's theme are a little more difficult to spot than graphical banners and navigation icons. For many Web sites, the "look" is more important than any thing else (such as Web sites that are trying to sell something stylish). In these cases, designers often include big, beautiful graphics that serve no other purpose that to enhance the theme or "style" of the page.

When you are looking for graphics that are part of the Web page's content, you must ask, "Which graphics add to the *message* of the page?" To discover graphics that are thematic or stylistic, ask, "Which of these add to the 'look' or theme of the Web page?"

6 Find a Web page you like that uses graphics that are directly related to the Web site's theme. List the title of the Web page and its URL here, and briefly describe how theme-related graphics work:

Web page title: _____

Web page URL: _____

How are the images used? _____

7 Review your storyboard and rough sketches created in created in the last section. Have you learned anything in this activity that can help you improve your use of graphics on these pages? Are there any changes you would like to make? If so, describe these changes in your design document under a new heading called *Improving the Graphics*.

THINKING ABOUT TECHNOLOGY: DESIGN

Web pages are not the only media created by computers that use graphics. Magazines (and many books) are developed on computers. Look at the pages of a popular magazine. In articles, do the images tend to be part of the message, serve as user interface elements, or add to the theme? How about the use of graphics in advertisements? Do graphics on advertising pages tend to be part of the message, serve as user interface elements, or add to the theme?

Design Desk *Symbols*

Symbols are more abstract than representations. A symbol is a graphic that represents something, but doesn't necessarily act like or look like the thing it represents. Sometimes the thing represented is an abstract thing like an idea. For example, a stop sign doesn't look like "stop," it symbolizes it.

Imagine you were making a Web site devoted to Shakespeare's plays. One way to organize the content is to divide the plays into three major types: comedies, tragedies, and histories. You might use the

classic laughing and crying Greek masks to indicate the tragedies and comedies. An icon of a book might be appropriate for the histories.

Because symbols are more abstract, there is the possiblility that they will be misunderstood. For that reason if the symbols are being used as buttons, you may want to include words to clarify the symbols. Symbols are most often used user interface elements (like buttons).

Design Desk *Metaphors*

A simile or metaphor is when something is like something else. If you say a computer is like a brain, you're using a metaphor; what you mean is that the computer works like a brain. In software, a metaphor relates computer functions with something they act like in the real world.

A good example of a metaphor is the trash can icon or recycling icon on your computer. When you drag a file to that icon, it deletes the file. The use of a trash icon builds on things you know (what a trash can looks like, what happens to things that get thrown into it) to help you understand things you may not (that by deleting a file you are reassigning the memory space allocated to that file in a memory

table to represent free memory available for future storage use).

A good metaphor can apply to several things at once, like the Windows or Macintosh operating systems, which use a variety of metaphors combined into one large metaphor of an office (not only a recyling bin but a desktop where you work, folders to put things in, an hourglass or wrist watch to tell you to be patient and wait). Unfortunately, even the best metaphor breaks down (for instance, on a computer you use windows to hold documents that you are working on; in a real office you use real windows to look out of when you're trying to avoid work!).

Graphic metaphors are the hardest to create and use, but when they are used, they often communicate something about the theme.

SCOOP

What is Microsoft FrontPage and how can it help you create sizzling Web sites? Visit *www.microsoft.com* and learn more about it.

Graphic Design Fundamentals

For artists, designing graphics on a computer is very different from other media like watercolors or oil painting. Computer graphics use very different color schemes, and the images show only a limited amount of detail. On the other hand, Web graphics are usually bright, and if you like, the pictures can be animated to show movement. These differences are sometimes a challenge for an artist, but once he or she learns to use computer graphics development tools, Web graphics can be a lot of fun to create.

Color

Computers are based on **additive colors**, not the **subtractive colors** you learned about in grade school. With your elementary school crayons, every color you color on the page reflected less and less light—it *subtracts* light. With subtractive colors, the more you put on, the darker it gets. (Remember that ugly brown color that everyone seemed to create by mixing too many subtractive colors together?)

By contrast, with additive colors, the more you add, the brighter the image becomes. With additive colors you are *adding* more light as you add colors. Because computer images are displayed by combining different colors of light, it has different primary colors (which result in different color combinations).

The primary additive colors are red, green, and blue, or **RGB** as it's abbreviated. Here's a chart of primary and secondary additive color mixes (these are not the same as the subtractive color mixes you can make with paint, so it might take some time to remember the correct combinations):

red + green = yellow
red + blue = magenta (a bright purple color)
blue + green = cyan (a bright blue-green color)
red + green + blue = white

Pixels

Another way in which computer graphics are unique is the **pixel**. If viewed with a magnifying glass on your monitor, pixels look like little mosaics. The word pixel is short for "*pic*ture *el*ement," and it is the small, basically square dot on your monitor. Compared to paper-based print media, a computer screen has a very low level of **resolution** (that is, the number of pixels or dots in a given space is a very small number compared to the number of dots in the same space in a printed document).

Resolution is measured in dots per inch (dpi) or sometimes in pixels per inch (ppi). When creating graphics for computer monitors (as in Web pages), you should save all your pictures at a resolution of 72 dpi. (On a Windows computer, you can use 96 dpi if you wish.) This resolution is what most computer monitors display, so putting in a Web graphic at 300 dpi, though it might look good on paper, is wasted on a Web page because the monitor displays it at 72 dpi anyway.

Because of the low resolution, something that looks very clear on paper often looks somewhat jagged or blurry on a computer screen. Because pixels are square, it's very difficult to display things like curves or diagonal lines without them appearing to be like little stair steps, as in Figure 8.2a. This jaggedness is called **aliasing**.

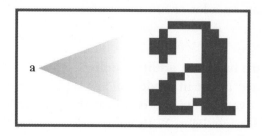

Figure 8.2a
The letter "a" showing aliasing

To fix this, sometimes the pixels around an object on the screen are colored with colors that are "between" the object and the background. This makes them look smoother, but a closer look makes them look blurred instead of stair-stepped (see Figure 8.2b). This process of using colors to fool the eye into thinking something is smooth is called **anti-aliasing**.

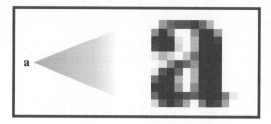

Figure 8.2b
The letter "a" showing anti-aliasing

Palettes

Computers are based entirely on binary numbers. Binary refers to the way computers count—by twos. Because of this, most native computer numbers are not based on tens, but on powers of two. For example, 2^8 (two to the power of eight) is the number 256. When a picture has a **color depth** of 8 bits (sometimes called bit depth), only 256 different colors can be represented. The collection of 256 specific colors in a certain order is called a **palette**.

Put another way, that means that each pixel on the screen can only be one of 256 specific colors found on the palette.

The tricky part about palettes is *which* 256 colors to use. Windows has one "standard" palette of 256, and Macintosh uses another, different "standard" palette of 256 colors. To be safe, Netscape has created a third, "standard" palette of "Web-safe" colors. This palette is actually only 216 colors, so Web designers can define some of their own colors. (See Appendix A for more information on Web-safe colors.)

Chapter 8 The Whys and Wherefores of Web Graphics

A palette of 16-bit color depth would have 2^{16} (two to the power of sixteen) colors or 65,526 different colors (called simply thousands of colors on the Macintosh). A 24-bit color palette would have 2^{24} (two to the power of twenty-four) or 16,777,216 colors (called simply millions of colors on the Macintosh). Unless you know that *all* your viewers are going to have computers with the ability to display thousands or millions of colors, it is best to use Netscape's 216 safe colors on your Web page graphics.

Dithering

A way to make up for the small numbers of colors in some palettes is **dithering**. If two dots of different colors are small enough, when your eye sees them together it will see only one color that is "in between" the two. In other words, if you put a red pixel next to a blue pixel on a black screen, it will look like a magenta (bright purple) dot.

Computers use this to trick your eyes into seeing colors that aren't really there by placing other colors next to each other to give the effect. These are usually placed in a pattern. This is called dithering, and it is a way to make the 256 colors in an 8-bit color palette seem like a lot more.

1 Imagine that you were trying to explain about computer graphics to a friend. To help you explain a few of these difficult concepts, write short, single-paragraph answers to each of the following questions. Use the material above to help you write your answers.
   - How are computer colors are different from printed colors?
   - What resolution should you use for Web-based graphics?
   - What palette should you use for Web pages, and why would you use this palette?
   - What are two tricks to make computer graphics seem like more than they are?

2 Cut construction paper of at least three different colors, into small squares. Now, carefully experiment with putting these squares together into patterns to make them "appear" to be different colors. Each small square is the equivalent of a "pixel." Because the squares are large, you may need to paste them onto a piece of black paper and set them across the room to see the color effect. (Black paper may make the picture look darker, but it won't change the color value—that's what computer monitors do.)

THINKING ABOUT TECHNOLOGY: YOUR CHOICE

The fact is, the best way to understand the concepts above is not to read about them but to play with them in a graphics program like Photoshop or a similar program like PaintShop Pro. With what you know about computers, what do you want to create for your Web site using a program like Photoshop?

ACTIVITY

8.3

Objective:

In this lesson, you'll learn to convert GIF and JPEG graphics.

Making Graphics

There are two graphics formats common on the Web: **GIF** and **JPEG** (sometimes written JPG). To use these two formats, it is important that you know a little about them.

CompuServe's Graphic Interchange Format—GIF

GIF (which stands for Graphic Interchange Format) was developed by an online company called CompuServe to send graphics over telecommunication lines to their subscribers. A GIF has the following characteristics:

- It is compressed or made smaller to make these graphics easy to transmit over the Web.

- The picture must be in 8-bit color (256 colors).

- Because it was the first inline graphic format used, it is the most compatible with older browsers.

- GIF pictures can appear in phases—with a low-resolution picture appearing first, then a higher-resolution, then a highest. This is very appealing to Web designers because it lets the user know that a picture is coming, and roughly what it will look like very early in the download.

- GIF pictures can be used to create simple animations; that is, they can change pictures over time so that they appear to move. This makes the files relatively large, so GIF animations are usually created with four or five pictures that are looped (played over and over again). Animated GIFs can be real eye-catchers!

- Parts of GIF-formatted pictures can be made transparent so they work over the top other pictures and backgrounds.

When images are physically small in size and simple in color make-up, GIF is the best choice. Therefore, they are especially useful for small, simple graphics like buttons, logos, and other simple interface graphics. Also, when compatibility with older browsers is important, GIFs are the only choices.

You may have software that you are using to create graphics. Many graphics programs can create GIF images. Some of these programs have very few options, others provide the artist with lots of options.

In this activity, we will demonstrate the graphic conversion process with Adobe Photoshop. Photoshop is one of the most popular graphic programs for computers, and it is available for both Windows and Macintosh computers. Some of the steps below may not be available in your software, or they may appear differently. As you learn your own graphic software, you will become more aware of its power and its limitations.

1. Open a graphic or a picture in Photoshop or in your own software. For this exercise, you can choose almost any graphic—clip art, small photograph, a logo, whatever.

2 Under the Image menu, select Mode; this will bring up another menu from which you should select Indexed Color... (see Figure 8.3a).

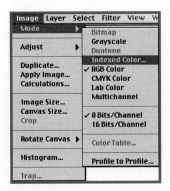

Figure 8.3a
The menus for changing an image to 256 colors in Photoshop

3 In the dialog box that comes up, select Web from the pop-up list for Palettes, and whether you want dithering or not (generally, if the picture is a photograph, you do); see Figure 8.3b. When you click on OK, the picture will be reduced to the 8-bit Web palette.

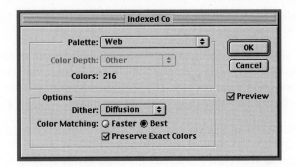

Figure 8.3b
Selecting a palette for changing an image to 256 colors

4 Pull down the File menu and choose Save As... A dialog box like the one in Figure 8.3c will appear. Use the pull-down list (like the one near the bottom of the figure) to choose GIF format (Photoshop calls it CompuServe GIF). Navigate to the same directory as the Web page that uses this graphic, or to a special graphics directory on your Web site. Give your file a name that ends in ".gif" and click on OK to save it.

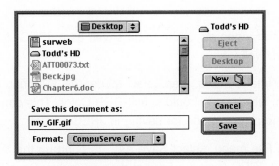

Figure 8.3c
Saving your reduced-color picture in Photoshop

The Joint Photographer's Expert Group Format—JPEG

Starting with Netscape Navigator version 3 and the release of Microsoft's Internet Explorer browser, another format became common for inline display of graphics. It is the JPEG format (pronounced jay-peg). JPEG was developed by the Joint Photographer's Expert Group, and the format took on the initials of the group that developed it. JPEG was originally developed to save space when storing and displaying photographs while still letting them look good. It was not specifically developed for use on the Web, but the Web provided the perfect medium for use of this format. The JPEG format has the following characteristics:

- Because it is designed to show off photographs well, 8-bit (256-color) graphics are not allowed; pictures must start in RGB format (which is one way to represent millions of colors).

- Unlike GIF, where there is only one level of compression, JPEG allows various compression and quality levels. Obviously, the more a picture is compressed, the less attractive it will be, and vice versa. On a scale of 1 to 10, 1 is the lowest quality with the most compression; 10 represents the highest quality with the least compression. Most people cannot tell a picture compressed at 10 from the original. A good compression level to start with is 6 or 7.

- Another difference between this format and GIF is that there is no transparency. This means that it is often not a good choice for buttons and other screen interface elements. Also, JPEG graphics currently cannot animate as easily as GIF files can.

- This format is not particularly good at compressing physically small graphics. In fact, even though JPEG is a more sophisticated format that GIF, a small graphic compressed in both is often smaller in GIF than in JPEG. A large, complex graphic, like a photograph, for example, is usually much better compressed using JPEG, and the result is much more attractive. For this reason it is considered best for large photographs and artwork.

- JPEG requires browsers newer than Netscape and IE version 3.

- Most professional graphics programs (like Adobe Photoshop) support JPEG as an option.

Next, we'll show you how to create a JPEG image, again using Photoshop.

1 In Photoshop, open an image to be saved as a JPEG. A photograph would work well.

2 Select the Image menu, then select Mode; this will bring up another menu from which you should select RGB Color. This converts your image into the proper mode for saving in JPEG format.

3 Under the File menu, select Save As... to bring up the Save As dialog box. Select JPEG from the Format drop-down list. Save the file with a simple name ending in .jpg or .jpeg (see Figure 8.3d). Click on Save.

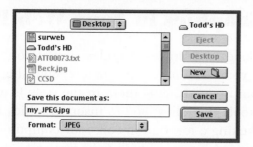

Figure 8.3d
The Save As... dialog box in Photoshop

④ After clicking on Save, the JPEG Options dialog box pops up. JPEG can save on a scale of quality levels. These levels are usually on a 10-point scale where 1 is the smallest, but least attractive, and 10 is the largest, but best looking. Choose a 6 or a 7 to start with. The JPEG options dialog box in Photoshop looks like Figure 8.3e.

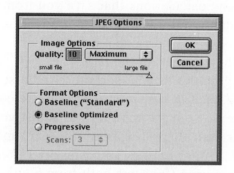

Figure 8.3e
The JPEG Options dialog box in Photoshop

⑤ Place the file in the same directory as the Web page that uses it or in a special graphics directory on your Web site.

THINKING ABOUT TECHNOLOGY: GRAPHICS TOOLS

You have learned a little bit about Photoshop in this activity. What other kinds of software tools and hardware tools and technologies are required to create large, photographic, and other important graphics that can add to the theme and message of a Web site?

Design Desk *Helper Applications and Plug-ins*

Nearly all browsers in multitasking operating systems (like Windows and Macintosh) have the ability to use helper applications. Helper applications are opened when a file format the browser cannot display is received. The browser calls on these other applications to attempt to show the file being transmitted. This will work with nearly any kind of file (for instance, you can even download a Microsoft Word document that will then automatically open Microsoft Word for you), but it is especially useful for graphic formats other than GIF and JPEG. There are "players" for nearly every format. The disadvantage to using helper applications is that these pictures will appear outside the browser window—they cannot be directly associated with the content of the page. You cannot tell where the other window is going to be located, or what's going to happen to it when you change what's in your browser's window.

Another capability available since version 2 browsers is the ability to use plug-ins, which are small pieces of computer code which, when placed in a particular folder near the browser software, act like they are part of the browser. This ability permits plug-ins to display many other formats "inline," among other things. One of the most popular plug-ins is QuickTime from Apple Computers. QuickTime allows digital video movies to be played inline on your browser's screen. The newest version also permits a plethora of graphic formats to be displayed. Another popular plug-in is Shockwave, which allows a kind of interactive vector graphic to be displayed.

ACTIVITY

8.4

Objective:

In this lesson, you will learn how to insert a graphic in your Web page.

Placing Graphics in Your Web Page

All this knowledge of graphics is useless if you don't know how to insert them into your Web page. Fortunately, choosing and creating graphics is the hard part. Placing them in the page is easy. Today there are many tools that allow you to insert graphics into a Web page easily by clicking a few buttons on your computer, then sizing the graphic or moving it around with your mouse to the correct position. Microsoft FrontPage is an example of this kind of Web site development software, but you can also create your Web pages in Microsoft Word, WordPerfect, HomePage, or other Web authoring tools.

These software tools automatically add HTML tags to your Web page and make many calculations that save you from worrying about the HTML tags, values, and numbers used in creating the page. These tools free you up to worry about the proportion and balance of your graphics as they appear on the page.

However, with graphics, it is important to understand what is happening in the code itself in case you need to make corrections to the HTML tags, or in case your software fails to adjust your graphics in the exact way you want them to appear. (To learn more about HTML tags, review *HTML Programming Concepts: Brief Course* or *HTML & JavaScript Programming Concepts* both from South-Western Educational Publishing.)

To place a graphic in your Web page using HTML tags, follow these easy steps:

1. Open the HTML document in which you wish to insert the graphic.

2. Place your cursor in the text where you want the graphic to appear. For instance, if it needs to appear beside a certain paragraph, set your cursor at the beginning of that paragraph, outside any other tags.

3. Type in the following tag:

   <IMG SRC="*filename*">

   Replace *filename* with the name of your file. That's all there is to it. (Note: If your graphic file is saved somewhere other than the same directory the HTML file is in, you may need to insert a complete path between the quotation marks, such as <IMG SRC="http://www.myserver.com/graphics/filename">.)

4. You can also change the size of graphics by adding HEIGHT and WIDTH tags like this.

   <IMG SRC="*filename*" HEIGHT=100 WIDTH=150>

5. You can increase the size and dimensions of the graphic by altering the numbers.

   <IMG SRC="*filename*" HEIGHT=200 WIDTH=225>

6 You may want to use alignment attributes to get the graphic to line up properly. Alignment attributes are added into the tag like HEIGHT and WIDTH above. They look like this:

<IMG SRC="*filename*" HEIGHT=200 WIDTH=225 ALIGN="TOP">

Designers (and some Web editor programs) use tables extensively to get images to align properly. Table tags are beyond the scope of this book, but you can learn more about it in the books *HTML Programming Concepts: Brief Course* or *HTML & JavaScript Programming Concepts* both from South-Western Educational Publishing, mentioned above.

THINKING ABOUT TECHNOLOGY: EXACT PLACEMENT

Web designers use tables, or numerical grids, to place graphics in the exact position they want them to appear on the page. Why is it sometimes important to have precise control over where Web pages will appear?

There are many ways to make animations and interactions in Web pages. JavaScript is a very popular tool. Use an Internet Search tool and learn more about JavaScript.

Net Ethics — RESPECT the Web: T = The Totally Cool Test

The Web prides itself on being creative, innovative, and exciting—in two words, *totally cool*. One of the great values of the Web is that people can see what other people have invented on the Web. This creates a great deal of competition to see who can come up with a "better Web page."

The competitive atmosphere of the Web is tempered by the fact that Web top publishers are normally happy to share their secrets with others. As the authors of this book, we have never met a Webmaster who wasn't willing to answer the few questions or to give a few suggestions. This sharing is assisted by the View Source option on your browser. This allows you to see how other Web page designers have created their pages.

While it is okay to get a few ideas, and it is totally cool to share, is not ethical or legal to simply copy and paste or steal HTML code or Web page graphics directly from a Web page without the express written permission of the Web publisher. Whereas your goal is to make your Web pages and Web sites totally cool, it is also unethical to steal ideas or without giving credit where credit is due.

Animated GIFs are fun and widely available on the Web. Use your Internet search tool to find a site that will let you download animated GIF files to use in your Web page creations.

WEB VOCABULARY

Define the following terms:

1. inline graphics
2. icons
3. additive color
4. subtractive color
5. RGB

6. pixel
7. resolution
8. aliasing
9. anti-aliasing
10. color depth

11. palette
12. dithering
13. GIF
14. JPEG

WEB REVIEW

Give a short answer to the following questions:

1. Why are inline graphics important in the history of the Web?

2. What conditions would justify the use of a very large graphic on a Web page?

3. When would you wish to use a photographic-like image on a Web page?

4. Explain why you might wish to use anti-aliasing in your graphics.

5. How are computer colors different from printed colors?

WEB SITE ⟋⟋⟋⟋ | Under Construction | ⟋⟋⟋⟋

It is now time to finalize your Web site. Apply what you know about graphics and add the necessary pictures to your Web pages. Combine your graphics with the text you created for your Web pages in Chapter 7.

WEB SITE ⟋⟋⟋⟋ | Under Construction Work Teams Ahead | ⟋⟋⟋⟋

Don't work alone! There is a lot that you may not know how to do—especially when it comes to integrating graphics into your site. Others on your team may be able to show you a trick or two.

Take your completed Web site to your team and have them evaluate your blending of text and graphics. Work as a team to foster constructive criticism and help each other make meaningful changes.

Perhaps the team can work together to edit and improve one Web site project at a time. Then the entire team can move to the next project, and the next, until every member of the team has an outstanding individual Web site.

WRITING ABOUT TECHNOLOGY: Planning Your Graphics

With what you know about Web design to this point, write a 100-word answer to one of the following options:

Option 1. What is the difference between subtractive and additive colors?

Option 2. What is a pixel and how can pixels be manipulated to display more colors than what actually exists on a color palette?

_____

_____

_____

_____

_____

_____

_____

_____

_____

_____

_____

_____

_____

Understanding RGB and Hexadecimal for Web-Safe Colors

What Is Hexadecimal?

Computers are binary devices. That means that they deal most easily with numbers that are powers of two. For example, at a fundamental level 2, 4, 8, 16, 32, and so on, are handled much more easily that the decimal numbers we are used to: 1, 10, 100, 1,000, and so on, which are powers of ten.

In order to accommodate this preference for powers of two, computers sometimes use a different numbering scheme from base 10. One common scheme is base 16. The technical term for base 16 is *hexadecimal*.

To write hexadecimal numbers, use the digits 0 through 9 for the numbers zero through nine, pretty much as in regular form. After that, we need some kind of single-digit characters to represent numbers 10 through 15. Computer scientists have substituted the letters A through F for those numbers. Therefore, counting to 15 in hexadecimal is: 1, 2, 3, 4, 5, 6, 7, 8, 9, A, B, C, D, E, and F.

In a normal decimal system, the first column of numbers is the "ones" column, and the second the "tens" column; in a hexadecimal system, the first column is the "ones" column, and the second is the "sixteens" column. When you count in hexadecimal, you count up to 15 (using letters from A thru F for the extra digits). When you reach sixteen, put a 1 in the "sixteens" column and start the "ones" column over. So counting to 27 in hexadecimal would look like this: 1, 2, 3, 4, 5, 6, 7, 8, 9, A, B, C, D, E, F, 10, 11, 12, 13, 14, 15, 16, 17, 18, 19, 1A, 1B. The hexadecimal "number" 1B equals the decimal number 27.

Numbers counting from 0 to 255 in decimal are shown in both decimal and hexadecimal form, with decimal on the left and hexadecimal on the right in the table on the next page.

0 = 00	32 = 20	64 = 40	96 = 60	128 = 80	160 = A0	192 = C0	224 = E0
1 = 01	33 = 21	65 = 41	97 = 61	129 = 81	161 = A1	193 = C1	225 = E1
2 = 02	34 = 22	66 = 42	98 = 62	130 = 82	162 = A2	194 = C2	226 = E2
3 = 03	35 = 23	67 = 43	99 = 63	131 = 83	163 = A3	195 = C3	227 = E3
4 = 04	36 = 24	68 = 44	100 = 64	132 = 84	164 = A4	196 = C4	228 = E4
5 = 05	37 = 25	69 = 45	101 = 65	133 = 85	165 = A5	197 = C5	229 = E5
6 = 06	38 = 26	70 = 46	102 = 66	134 = 86	166 = A6	198 = C6	230 = E6
7 = 07	39 = 27	71 = 47	103 = 67	135 = 87	167 = A7	199 = C7	231 = E7
8 = 08	40 = 28	72 = 48	104 = 68	136 = 88	168 = A8	200 = C8	232 = E8
9 = 09	41 = 29	73 = 49	105 = 69	137 = 89	169 = A9	201 = C9	233 = E9
10 = 0A	42 = 2A	74 = 4A	106 = 6A	138 = 8A	170 = AA	202 = CA	234 = EA
11 = 0B	43 = 2B	75 = 4B	107 = 6B	137 = 8B	171 = AB	203 = CB	235 = EB
12 = 0C	44 = 2C	76 = 4C	108 = 6C	139 = 8C	172 = AC	204 = CC	236 = EC
13 = 0D	45 = 2D	77 = 4D	109 = 6D	140 = 8D	173 = AD	205 = CD	237 = ED
14 = 0E	46 = 2E	78 = 4E	110 = 6E	141 = 8E	174 = AE	206 = CE	238 = EE
15 = 0F	47 = 2F	79 = 4F	111 = 6F	142 = 8F	175 = AF	207 = CF	239 = EF
16 = 10	48 = 30	80 = 50	112 = 70	143 = 90	176 = B0	208 = D0	240 = F0
17 = 11	49 = 31	81 = 51	113 = 71	145 = 91	177 = B1	209 = D1	241 = F1
18 = 12	50 = 32	82 = 52	114 = 72	146 = 92	178 = B2	210 = D2	242 = F2
19 = 13	51 = 33	83 = 53	115 = 73	147 = 93	179 = B3	211 = D3	243 = F3
20 = 14	52 = 34	84 = 54	116 = 74	148 = 94	180 = B4	212 = D4	244 = F4
21 = 15	53 = 35	85 = 55	117 = 75	149 = 95	181 = B5	213 = D5	245 = F5
22 = 1	54 = 36	86 = 56	118 = 76	150 = 96	182 = B6	214 = D6	246 = F6
23 = 1	55 = 37	87 = 57	119 = 77	151 = 97	183 = B7	215 = D7	247 = F7
24 = 1	56 = 38	88 = 58	120 = 78	152 = 98	184 = B8	216 = D8	248 = F8
25 = 1	57 = 39	89 = 59	121 = 79	153 = 99	185 = B9	217 = D9	249 = F9
26 = 1	58 = 3A	90 = 5A	122 = 7A	154 = 9A	186 = BA	218 = DA	250 = FA
27 = 1	59 = 3B	91 = 5B	123 = 7B	155 = 9B	187 = BB	219 = DB	251 = FB
28 = 1	60 = 3C	92 = 5C	124 = 7C	156 = 9C	188 = BC	220 = DC	252 = FC
29 = 1	61 = 3D	93 = 5D	125 = 7D	157 = 9D	189 = BD	221 = DD	253 = FD
30 = 1	62 = 3E	94 = 5E	126 = 7E	158 = 9E	190 = BE	222 = DE	254 = FE
31 = 1	63 = 3F	95 = 5F	127 = 7F	159 = 9F	191 = BF	223 = DF	255 = FF

What Does Hexadecimal Numbering Have to Do with Color?

As stated, computers deal in binary numbers. So, representation of color on a computer is also in binary numbers.

To represent the 16-million-plus colors that the human eye can distinguish, computer scientists have come up with a clever scheme that connects the hexadecimal numbers above to each of the three primary additive colors (see Chapter 8), red, green, and blue (RGB for short).

Imagine three dials or knobs, one for each color (see Figure A.1). As you turn the dial to the right, it represent a higher number. As you turn it to the left, a lower number. The numbers are between 0 and 255 (or, in hexadecimal, between 0 and FF).

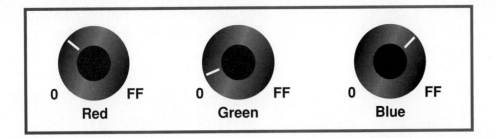

With these three imaginary knobs, you can create any color. For example, to create a pure red, you simply turn the Red knob all the way up (to FF) and the other two all the way down (to 00). To create a pure blue, turn the Blue knob all the way to the right (FF) and the other two knobs all the way to the left (00).

What if you wanted a darker blue? Just turn the Blue knob down a little, and you have a darker color.

What about white? Turn all three knobs to all the way up to "FF."

How about if you wanted yellow? As mentioned in Chapter 8, in additive colors, yellow is a product of adding red and green. Therefore, turn the Red and Green knobs all the way up to the right, and the Blue knob all the way down to the left, and you have yellow.

Using RGB with hexadecimal numbers is exactly how the Web designates colors. Except, instead of turning knobs, you put six hexadecimal digits all in a row preceded by a pound sign (#) to show that it's a number. Then, the first two digits represent red, the second two, green, and the third two digits are blue. So for pure red, you would type: "#FF0000." For pure blue you would type: "#0000FF," and for pure green you would type: "#00FF00." Now, "#FFFF00" would give you a pure yellow.

What Are "Web-Safe" Colors?

If all the computers in the world could handle millions of colors, this would work perfectly. Unfortunately, there are many that can only display 256 colors. So, just to be safe, we'll select 256 of the millions of possible colors for use on the Web. (Actually, we're only going to select 216—we'll save the other "color slots" for designers to add their own colors.)

How do we choose? Netscape came up with a simple trick to decide which colors to choose. They use *only* doubled numbers that are divisible by three in each of the positions (R, G, and B). These number are:

00   33   66   99   CC   FF

(In decimal numbers, these values would be: 0, 51, 102, 153, 204, and 255. See the table above.) This gives you six choices for each primary color: red, green, and blue. That means that instead of having 256 x 256 x 256 (= 16,777,216) different colors, you only have 6 x 6 x 6 (= 216) different colors. This 216 possible colors are the "safe" colors.

Can you tell which of the numbers below are "Web-safe" colors, and which are not?

#3366CC   #000077   #FFFF33   #DDCC33

(Extra credit: what colors do you think these represent?)

The best way to see these colors is to try them out in your HTML code. Use the rule above to change the background color of a Web page and view it in your browser to see the colors. The background color is modified by adding the a "BGCOLOR=" argument to your body tag, like this:

<BODY BGCOLOR="FFFF00">

The tag above would make the background bright yellow.

<BODY BGCOLOR="99FF99">

The above tag would make a light, pastel green (the addition of the other two colors, red and blue, in equal amounts adds "white" to the color, making it lighter.)

Try your own combinations.

Glossary of HTML

The following glossary is not a complete set for HTML. It is provided here as a convenience for identifying some of the most common HTML terms.

HTML is the set of tags and other entities used to "mark up" a document for display on a Web browser.

In the glossary, tags are listed with their purpose or meaning. Some common attributes may also be listed. The tags are organized into types of tags (not alphabetically), which assumes that you know something about tags and the structure of an HTML document.

Basic HTML Syntax

HTML Tag Format

HTML tags are always written inside angle brackets (< and >). Angle brackets are nothing more that the less than and greater than symbols, commonly typed by pressing shift-comma and shift-period.

Tag Pairs

HTML tags most often appear in pairs, with an opening tag and a closing tag. The closing tag contains a forward slash character just inside the angle brackets, like this:

</B>

The opening tag turns the desired function on; the closing tag turns the function off. For example, the <B> tag is used to make something boldface. The word *content* in the example below would be set in boldface:

This is the <B>content</B>

Some tags do not require closing tags; on some tags, the closing tag is optional. For example, both of the following markups are correct:

<P>This is a new paragraph.</P>

<P>This is a new paragraph.

Nesting Tags

When multiple tags apply to the same material, they should be "nested" properly. Nesting refers to turning functions off in the opposite order from the way which they were turned on.

A simple way to tell if tags are properly nested is to draw lines between opening and closing tags. If the lines cross, they are wrong. If not, they are correctly nested.

In the example below, the one on the left is improperly nested, and the one on the right is correct:

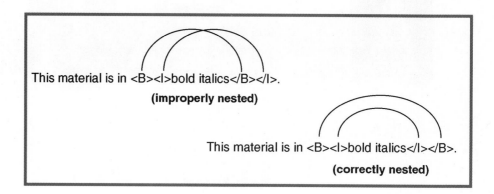

This material is in <B><I>bold italics</B></I>.
(improperly nested)

This material is in <B><I>bold italics</I></B>.
(correctly nested)

Figure B.1
Nesting schemes in HTML

Document Tags

A standard HTML document contains tags that identify parts of the document itself. These are <HEAD> and <BODY>. Those items between the opening and closing <HEAD> tag are not displayed in the user's browser, but are read by it and used in other ways. The content between the <BODY> tags are displayed in the browser window, if possible.

One of the most common elements of the <HEAD> is the <TITLE> tag, which appears in the browser window's title (above the window—not in the window itself).

Surrounding both of these are the <HTML> tags that identify the entire document as being HTML. The typical arrangement for an HTML document is as follows (they have been indented to make them easier to follow):

```
<HTML>
    <HEAD>
            <TITLE>The Window Title</TITLE>
    </HEAD>
    <BODY>
            [The page's content goes here...]
    </BODY>
</HTML>
```

Tag Attributes

Many tags can contain attributes. Attributes are added to the opening tag, but not the closing tag. (If you are turning the function off with a closing tag, you are presumably turning off all its attributes as well.)

Attributes are specific to the tag (you can't just make them up, and you can't just use one that works in one tag and make it work in another). Also, some attributes have values, and some do not. (Tag attribute values are usually shown by an equal sign following the attribute, and the value in quotation marks).

Attributes appear inside the angle brackets of the opening tag, like this:

```
<BODY BGCOLOR="#FFFFFF">
</BODY>
```

In this instance, the tag (<BODY>) contains an attribute (BG-COLOR=) which has a value ("#FFFFFF"). This combination turns the background color of the page to white. (See Appendix A for an explanation of hexadecimal numbers and colors.)

Tag Glossary

In the heading for each tag, the words to the right refer to whether the tag takes a closing tag and whether the tag has attributes, like this.

Text Breaks, Lines, and Layout

\<P\>   **Paragraph**   **Optional closing tag**   **Takes attributes**

The equivalent of putting two returns after a paragraph; leaves a blank line. The <P> tag has an optional closing tag (</P>). We recommend using the closing tag so that formatting attributes can be added to the opening tag. For example: <P ALIGN="RIGHT"> *Text*</P> will right-align the text between the tags.

\<BR\>   **Break**   **No closing tag**   **No attributes**

The line break tag is equivalent of putting one return after a paragraph: there is no blank line between paragraphs. The <BR> tag does not require a closing tag. Also, <BR> tags can be "stacked" or multiplied to cause multiple spaces between paragraphs.

\<HR\>   **Horizontal Rule**   **No closing tag**   **Takes attributes**

The terminology for this tag comes from the print industry where a line drawn in the text is called a rule. The <HR> tag does not require a closing tag. The tag can contain attributes that vary the width of the line drawn and whether there is a drop shadow or not (WIDTH="4" and NOSHADE, respectively).

Text Style Tags

Text styles fall into two categories: logical and physical. When the Web was first conceived, it's purpose was to share scientific papers. Consequently, many tags were created that were based on the logical structure of text, not the physical look. These logical tags allow the browser to determine how to display tagged text.

Physical tags, on the other hand, are more like the physical display characteristics of a typical word processor—based on how the text looks. All of the tags below fall into one of these two categories.

| `<ADDRESS>` | Address | Required closing tag | No attributes |

A logical text style (one for which the browser can choose how to display) for writing addresses. Usually this indents the text.

| `<B>` | Boldface | Required closing tag | No attributes |

A physical style for displaying the surrounded text in boldface.

| `<BLOCKQUOTE>` | Block quote | Required closing tag | No attributes |

A logical text style for large blocks of quoted material in a text. Usually this indents about half an inch in from both the right and left.

| `<CITE>` | Citation | Required closing tag | No attributes |

A logical text style for citations. Usually this puts the citation in italics.

| `<CODE>` | Computer code | Required closing tag | No attributes |

A logical text style intended to surround computer code. Usually this puts the text in a monospaced font, like Courier.

| `<EM>` | Emphasis | Required closing tag | No attributes |

A logical text style for giving emphasis to the surrounded text. Usually this puts the text into italics.

| `<FONT>` | Font | Required closing tag | Takes attributes |

A physical style for changing the font of the surrounded text. The attributes can include such tags as SIZE="+2" (make the surrounded text two sizes larger than default) and FACE="HELVETICA,GENEVA,SANSERIF" (use one of the identified font faces). This tag is generally not compatible with older browsers.

| `<I>` | Italics | Required closing tag | No attributes |

A physical style for displaying the surrounded text in italics.

| `<PRE>` | Preformatted | Required closing tag | No attributes |

A physical style for displaying the surrounded without any formatting changes. For example, all space characters and the return character are left intact. Usual this displays as a monospaced font (like Courier) as well.

| `<STRONG>` | Strong emphasis | Required closing tag | No attributes |

A logical text style for giving strong emphasis to the surrounded text. Usually this puts the text into boldface.

| `<TT>` | Teletype | Required closing tag | No attributes |

A physical style for displaying the surrounded text in a monospaced font like a teletype or typewriter.

| `<XMP>` | Example | Required closing tag | No attributes |

A logical text style for displaying HTML code in the browser window. This unique tag usually sets the text in a monospaced font (like Courier), but it also allows all characters which would normally be interpreted to be displayed, such as less than (<), greater than (>), ampersands (&), and so on.

Page Layout Tags

| `<CENTER>` | Center | Required closing tag | No attributes |

Though not strictly a text style tag, <CENTER> affects all the text between it and it's closing tag (</CENTER>) by centering it on the page. It has no attributes.

| `<H1>` | Level 1 Heading | Required closing tag | No attributes |

A top-level heading. Usually displayed at a large point size, bold-face.

| `<H2>` | Level 2 Heading | Required closing tag | No attributes |

A second level heading. Usually displayed at a large point size, boldface (but smaller than <H1>).

| `<H3>` through `<H6>` | Other headings | Required closing tag | No attributes |

Third- through sixth-level headings, each smaller that the previous.

| `<TABLE>` | Table | Required closing tag | Takes attributes |

The <TABLE> tag is used to surround text which is to be formatted as a table. Additional tags include:

| `<TR>` | Table Row | Required closing tag | Takes attributes |

Use the <TR> tag to surround things to be in the same row in a table. These should be inside a set of <TABLE> tags.

| `<TD>` | Table Cell | Required closing tag | Takes attributes |

Use the <TD> tag to surround each cell (or column) in a table. These should be inside a set of <TR> tags, which should be inside a set of <TABLE> tags.

Tables are powerful ways to lay out your Web pages attractively. For more information on using tables in HTML, use your favorite search engine to find sites related to "HTML tables," or check the Web page for this book at *webdesign.swep.com*.

Lists

Some of the most flexible and useful tags are those that allow you to create lists. Lists usually take two sets of tags, one to surround the entire list, and another to surround each of the items in the list.

Unless otherwise stated, the list item tag is <LI>, which has an optional closing tag and can take attributes (depending on the list type).

| <OL> | Ordered List | Required closing tag | Takes attributes |

The ordered list uses the <LI> tag on each item in the list. When displayed in the browser, a number is displayed at the beginning of each line referenced to the order in which they appear.

| <UL> | Unordered List | Required closing tag | Takes attributes |

An unordered list uses the <LI> tag on each item in the list. When displayed in the browser, a bullet (•) is displayed at the beginning of each line.

| <DL> | Definition List | Required closing tag | No attributes |

The definition list is a unique way to have the contents in the list vary between two different list item types. Use the tag <DT> for the "definition title" and <DD> for the "definition." This tag is particularly useful for glossarys, dictionaries, or other types of entries where you want indentation to show the relationship between items in the list.

Inline Graphics

| <IMG> | Image | Required closing tag | Takes attributes |

The <IMG> tag must have an attribute to identify the file name and location of the image to be displayed. This is done using the attribute SRC="*url*." In addition, other attributes (like HEIGHT="24" or WIDTH="322") are also possible. See the section on URLs, below, for more detail on how to use the URL in the quotation marks.

Anchors (Hyperlinks)

| <A> | Anchor (hyperlink) | Required closing tag | Takes attributes |

This is the tag that creates the most excitement. The text or graphic surrounded by <A> tags is "hot" and can be clicked to take the user to a new location on the Web. The location is determined by the contents of the attribute HREF="*url*"

| <A> | Anchor (target) | Required closing tag | Takes attributes |

There is a second use of the <A> tag that makes it the recipient (not the sender) of a link. Using the <A NAME="#anyname> tag, you can get to a specific place *within* an HTML document (not just to its top). When a URL contains a pound sign ("#"), the words after the pound sign are treated as the target of a link within an HTML document.

additive color: Color produced by illumination (as in that produced by the cathode ray tube used by most monitors). The primary additive colors are red, green, and blue (RGB). See also subtractive color.

aliasing: The inability of computer screens to accurately represent curves and diagonal lines, resulting in a "stair-stepped" look.

anchor tag: The kind of tag used to insert a hyperlink in HTML text. The syntax is <A HREF="server-name.com"> Hyperlinked text here</A>.

anti-aliasing: The selection of colors on curves and diagonal lines which blend with the background color to trick the eye into thinking aliased graphics are really smooth.

audience: The group to whom your Web site is designed to appeal. An audience will have something in common with or an interest in the topic of your Web site.

background: Things that you can assume your intended audience already knows. Identifying what your audience knows already can help you streamline your Web content.

balance: The placement of elements on a page in such a way as to make them look even across an imaginary center line. Balance can be symmetrical or asymmetrical.

banner: The title of a newspaper or Web site. Usually in large text, it is often a graphic rather than text on a Web page.

chunks: Information divided into logical pieces.

color depth: The number of computer bits used to represent colors in a graphic. An 8-bit color depth means that there is a palette of 256 colors possible. 16-bit color depth would have 2^{16} (two to the power of sixteen) colors or 65,526 different colors (called simply "thousands" on the Macintosh). 24-bit color would have 2^{24} (two to the power of twenty-four) or 16,777,216 colors (called simply "millions" on the Macintosh). Color depth is a function of the amount of memory allocated to displaying graphics on the computer.

color scheme: A plan about which color(s) would look good together in your Web site.

consistency errors: Errors in one's text due to change in verb tense, subject, inconsistent use of contractions, and so on. These kinds of errors are not caught by spell checkers and indicate poor communication skills on the part of the author.

containers: The term for the pair of HTML tags that surround text to indicate an attribute. For instance, <I> and </I> are the containers for italic text.

context device: An item of organization or structure in a communication medium that is used to identify parts or navigation through that medium. Page numbers and headings are examples of context devices used in paper media.

database: In the Web, a searchable, comprehensive list (including categorizations and topics) of Web pages and sites.

design: A kind of advanced planning for the purpose of guiding creative efforts.

design document: A detailed, written plan for your Web site, including your information, interaction, and presentation design decisions.

dithering: A way to make up for the small numbers of colors in some palettes. If two dots of different color are small enough, when your eye sees them together it will see only one color that is "in between" the two. Computers use this to trick your eye into seeing colors that aren't really there by placing other colors next to each other to give the effect. These are usually place in a kind of pattern. Dithering is a way to make the 256 colors in an 8-bit color palette seem like a lot more.

downloading: The act of moving information from one computer to another, as from a Web server to a Web browser.

end tag: In HTML, the tag that "turns off" a display instruction to the Web browser. It is identical to the start tag, with the addition of a slash to indicate the end of the attribute. For instance, when turning off italics, the close tag is </I>. See also start tag.

flowchart: A diagram that shows the relationships information chunks. Often used to determine the structure and flow of Web pages or other documents.

font: A typeface. On computers, the typeface family that has a similar look. Font choices can help make your Web page look attractive and be easily readable.

GIF: A compressed graphics format invented by CompuServe and used to transmit graphics over telecommunication lines, like the Web. GIFs have 8-bit color depth and was the first format used by Web browsers.

graphics: An element of artwork on a Web page. Graphics can include digitized photographs, clip art, icons, or other forms of artwork.

greeking: Substitution of straight or wavy lines in place of text on a thumbnail sketch or rough sketch.

grid: A series of vertical and horizontal lines used to guide the placement of elements in a layout. The lines are called guidelines or gridlines.

GUI (graphical user interface): A way for people to interact with computers. In a GUI (pronounced "gooey") commands are represented by icons and pull-down menus, which people use by clicking or dragging with a mouse or other pointing device.

hard-coding: The process of marking HTML text by hand, that is, not using an HTML editor or Web development software.

hierarchical structure: An information structure in which each item potential connects to two or more at a lower level, like a family tree. Probably the most common structure for informational Web sites as it helps organize the content.

home page: The main page of a Web site, the first ones your visitors will see; also called an index page or a welcome page.

HTML: Hypertext Markup Language; the language used to format Web pages so that they can be properly displayed in a Web browser.

HTML tags: The actual code that instructs a Web browser how to display a document. HTML tags consist of an open angle bracket, text, and a closed angle bracket, like <BR>.

HTTP: Hypertext Transfer Protocol, the protocol used by the Web to transport Web content.

hyperlink: A connection in one Web page to another Web document, usually activated by clicking on it with the mouse. In Microsoft Internet Explorer and Netscape Navigator, hyper-links are most often shown as text that is underlined and in another color, often blue.

icons: Small, often symbolic graphics used as buttons for links or functions.

information design: Information design is concerned with what you want to tell about (the message), to whom you're going to tell it (audience), what things they already know (background), why you want to tell it (purpose), and how the information will be structured.

inline graphic: Graphics and other media placed in a Web browser's window, directly onto the Web page.

interaction design: Interaction design is concerned with how the information will be organized on the page (organization), how people will find their way around your Web site (navigation), and how people will work with the information (interactivity) on your Web site.

interactivity: How the user will manipulate or use the information in your Web site.

Internet: The global network of computers used for communication. The Internet has many components, including email and FTP, but the Web is the largest and most popular part.

JPEG: A graphic format named after the group that invented it: the Joint Photographer's Expert Group. It uses pictures that are in millions of colors (24-bit) and has several levels of compression. An excellent format for photographs.

layout: How the elements of a Web page are physically organized on the screen.

linear structure: An information structure wherein parts are connected to each other in a straight line. Especially useful for content such as stories or step-by-step instruction.

logical style: A method of identifying how certain text is used, not necessarily how it looks. Logical styles in HTML include marking text to appear as a citation or with emphasis.

message: Your main topic, what your Web site will be about. The message should be tailored to the audience. The message includes all of your text and graphics.

mixed structure: A mixture of two or more different information structures.

modem: A device that allows computers to communicate over regular telephone lines. It does this by *modulat*ing the data into tones on one end and *dem*odulating the tones back into data on the other, hence the name "modem."

navigation: How the user will get around in your Web site. Good, easy navigation is critical to attracting an audience.

ordered list: In HTML, a list with sequentially numbered list items.

organization: How the Web site is put together or described; closely tied to the information structure.

packets: Small bundles of data on the Internet that are addressed with the recipient's Internet address so that they can be assembled into the appropriate content at the final location. Used when downloading data from one computer to another.

palette: A set of colors (usually 8-bit or 256 colors) used to depict a graphic. Windows and Macintosh both have "standard" 8-bit palettes, as does Netscape Navigator. It is also possible to have a palette that is colors selected from a graphic or multiple graphics.

physical style: A method of identifying specifically how text is displayed in HTML. Physical style includes indicating when text should appear as bold, underlined, or italic, among other things.

pixel: A single *pic*ture *el*ement. The basic part of a computer graphic.

place finding: A method of allowing your Web visitor to determine where they are in your site by using context devices; a kind of system of landmarks.

presentation design: Presentation design is planning how your new Web site will look—what colors will look good together on your site (color scheme), what fonts or styles of type you will use for the written part of your Web site, what graphics are needed, and how it will all be combined or arranged into a specific layout. (Sometimes called visual design.)

proportion: A balance among the parts, or elements of a Web page, or, the comparative relationship, harmony, balance, equilibrium, and measurement of elements on a Web page.

purpose: Why you want to tell your message. Common purposes for Web sites include sales, advertising, or simple information propagation.

random access structure: An information structure in which any part has access to any other part (and every other part) in a single connection. Only good for sites with limited numbers of pages or parts because the number of connections grows as new parts are added.

resolution: The number of pixels or dots in a certain space. Often measure in inches in dots per inch (dpi) or pixels per inch (ppi).

RGB: A format for computer graphics wherein each color is represented by 256 shades. In this way there can be 256 different shades of reds, 256 shades of green, and 256 shades of blue, making 256 x 256 x 256 (16,777,216) possible color combinations.

rough sketch: A roughly developed sketch, often based on a thumbnail sketch. Used to develop the look of a Web page or other graphic design.

scope: How much information a Web site covers.

search engine: A Web site with access to a database of Web sites that a user can search by entering keywords. The database may contain references to millions of Web pages. The results of the search are usually displayed as hyperlinks, which the user can click to see the Web pages found. See also Web index.

spider: An automatic program that "crawls" the Web looking for new Web pages and Web sites to add to a search engine's database.

start tag: In HTML, the start tag is the code that "turns on" a certain instruction to the browser. For instance, when marking up italic text, the start tag would be <I>. See also end tag.

storyboard: An elaborate, detailed flowchart in which each element of a project is represented as a card on a board. In the case of a Web site, each card on the board represents one of the Web pages in the site.

structure: How the information that makes up your message is put together or described (often illustrated using flowcharts).

subtractive color: Color produced by reflections (as in that produced on printed paper). See also additive color.

table of contents: A page listing the contents of a book, and by analogy, the contents of a Web site. See **home page**.

tags: Pairs of HTML code used to mark up regular text for display on the Web.

thumbnail sketches: A series of very small (usually one to two inches wide by an inch or so tall) rough sketches used to try out a lot of visual ideas. Used by graphic artists to test their ideas to get an idea of how they'll look. Often, many thumbnails are drawn, but only one or two are selected for further development into rough sketches.

tiled: In graphics, where an image is repeated in a pattern, like floor tile. The background of many Web pages used tiled graphics.

title page: The beginning page of a book, and, by analogy, of a Web site. See home page.

traffic: The number of people who visit a Web site in a particular time period.

unity: Using a common color or style to make elements on a page look like they belong together.

unordered list: In HTML, a list that identifies each list item with a bullet.

URL (Uniform Resource Locator): The unique address from which a Web document is called.

visual theme: A general concept, idea, or style around which all the visual elements of a Web page are based.

Web browser: Software used to retrieve, interpret, and display Web content over the Internet.

Web index: A Web site containing information about other Web sites that has been organized alphabetically or categorically to allow access to these sites by browsing and clicking on hyperlinks. See also search engine.

Web pages: A Web-delivered document. Web pages are text that has been marked up with HTML tags so that it displays properly in a Web browser.

Web server: A computer whose purpose is to deliver Web content over the Internet. The actual documents, graphics, and other materials that make up Web pages and Web sites reside on the server.

Web site: A collection of Web pages with a common theme or purpose.

welcome page: The starting point for your Web site; often known as the index page or the home page. It is the "front door" to the rest of the site.

white space: In publishing, the "empty" space around and between text that makes it more readable.

World Wide Web: Often nicknamed "WWW" or simply called "the Web." A service that uses the Internet to transmit hyperlinked documents.

Index

icons, 150
images or colors, 97
information design
  audience, 62-63
  described, 49-51, 150
  message, 60-61, 67-72
  parts of, 58-59
  purpose and scope, 64-66
inline graphic, 148, 150
interaction design
  described, 52-53, 150
  elements of, 75
  how users will navigate site, 82-85
  identifying the welcome page, 77-78
  organizing pages, 79-81
  place finding, 86-88
  storyboard, 76
interactivity, 52, 150
Internet, 3, 150
Internet portal sites, 75

JPEG (joint photographer's expert group), 132, 150
justifying text, 34-35

<KBD> tag, 31

<L> tag, 29
layout, 151
LIFO (last in first out), 19
line breaks, adding, 26
linear structure, 68, 77, 151
links and content, 97
lists, 35-37, 147-148
local links, 39-40
logical style, 29-33,151

Memex, 12
message, 50, 151
metaphor, 81, 126
mixed structure, 69, 151
modem, 9, 151
Mosaic, 10
motion capture, 79

National Center for Supercomputing (NCSA), 10
navigation, 52, 151
navigation controls, 84
navigating a site, 82-88
nesting tags, 143
Netscape, 10
  viewing a link in, 39
Netscape Communicator window, 6

ordered list, 35-37, 151
organization, 52, 151

<P> tag, 24
packets, 3, 151
page layout tags, 147
palette, 128, 151
paragraph ending tag, 24
paragraphs
  adding white space betweem 24-25
physical style, 29-30, 151
pixel, 127, 151
place finding, 86-88, 151
plagiarism, 106
plain text file, 21
plug-ins, 133
presentation design
  described, 54-55, 151
  organizing space using a grid, 100-102

  rough sketches, 92-94
  thumbnail sketches, 92
  user interface, 97-99
  visual design, 91
  visual theme, 95-96
proportion, 101, 151
pronoun use, 113
purpose, 64, 151
purpose test, 88

random access structure, 67-68, 151
relative URL, 40
representations, 124
resolution, 127, 151
resource designing, 94
RGB, 127, 151
rough sketch, 92-94, 151

<SMALL> tag, 29
<SUB> tag, 29
<SUP> tag, 29
scope, 65, 151
search engine, 5, 151
sidebar, 98
Spell Check, 118
spider, 108, 152
start tag, 18, 152
storyboard, 76, 152
structure, 50, 152
styles
  logical, 30-33
  physical, 29-30
subheading, 98
subtractive color, 127, 152
symbols, 126

<TT> tag, 29
table of contents, 83, 152
tag attributes, 144
tag glossary, 145
tag pairs, 143
tags, 17, 152
text
  centering and justifying, 34-35
  converting plain text files to HTML files, 15, 18